RETIREMENT is

Recess

for Grown-Ups

RETIREMENT is

Recess

for Grown-Ups

When the bell rings will your be ready?

JIM COLLIER

Swing Tree Press ™

Retirement is Recess for Grown-Ups: When the Bell Rings Will You be Ready?
Published by Swing Tree Press
Larkspur, CO

Publisher's Cataloging-in-Publication data

Names: Collier, James Ward, author.
Title: Retirement is recess for grown-ups: when the bell rings will you be ready?
 / Jim Collier.
Description: First trade paperback original edition. | Larkspur [Colorado] : Swing Tree Press, 2019. Also available as an ebook.
Identifiers: ISBN 978-0-9981174-2-3
Subjects: LCSH: Finance, Personal. | Retirement--Planning.
BISAC: PERSONAL FINANCE / Retirement Planning.
Classification: LCC HQ1062.R873 | DDC 332.024014–dc22

QUANTITY PURCHASES: Schools, companies, professional groups, clubs, and other organizations may qualify for special terms when ordering quantities of this title. For information, email jim@retirementrecess.com.

Proof of Purchase Code: RECESS

Swing Tree Press ™

This book is dedicated to my life partner, spouse,
and retirement-recess playmate—Carol.
Your daily support of all my dreams and aspirations
encourages me to seek greater things.
Thank you for being my number one fan.

Table of Contents

Introduction   15

Retirement is Recess for Grown-Ups.   17
When the Recess Bell Rings, Will You Be Ready?

Chapter 1 The Evolution of Retirement—   25
           How We Got to Where We Are

Chapter 2 The Retirement-Income Stool   35

Chapter 3 Not Ready for Retirement Recess   57

Chapter 4 The Great American Default Retirement Plan—   79
           "I'll Just Keep Working"

Chapter 5 Planning for Retirement Recess   85

Chapter 6 Financial Planning—Science or Art?   91

Chapter 7 Creating Your Future Life Plan   95

Chapter 8 Strategies for Moving into Retirement   117

Chapter 9 Recess Ready   129

Chapter 10 The Real Risk   133

Chapter 11 Risk—Cause and Effect   135

Chapter 12 Retirement Income Security Killers (RISK)   139

Chapter 13 Managing RISK before and during retirement years 187

Chapter 14 Hiring a Lifetime Financial Adviser   201

Chapter 15 Funding and Protecting Your   231
            Retirement-Life Plan

Chapter 16 Planning for the Journey: 261
            One-Way or Round-Trip Ticket?

Conclusion: A Retirement-Recess Life Well Lived   273

Disclaimer

This book contains the ideas, thoughts and opinions of its author, Jim Collier. Neither the author or publisher is engaged in rendering legal, tax, investment, insurance, financial or accounting advice. The strategies outlined in this book may not be suitable for every individual, and are not guaranteed or warranted to produce any particular results. A competent professional should be consulted if such services or advice is required.

No warranty is made with respect to the accuracy or completeness of the information contained herein. Both the author and publisher specifically disclaim any responsibility for any liability, loss or risk, personal or otherwise which is incurred as a result, directly or indirectly, of the use and application of any of the contents of this book.

Although reference is made to broad investment indexes such as the S&P 500 stock index, the author and publisher neither endorse or recommend the utilization of any specific investment index or any other investment allocation as a promoted investment choice. Investment index references are for illustration purposes only.

Persons described in this book are fictional characters unless otherwise disclosed. Any similarity to real people is coincidental.

Preface

Insomuch as I have tried to encapsulate what I feel are important topics relating to the preparation of a successful retirement lifestyle, I certainly cannot claim this work to be all-inclusive on a topic as broad as "retirement planning." To do so would require more pages than the average reader would wish to absorb from one book. For example, some readers may be planning on generating retirement income from real estate rental properties or small-business income during their retirement years. Although both of these income generators are viable means to securing financial independence, in the interests of space, I have chosen to keep the primary focus for generating retirement income on financial assets. Additionally, there are also those who aspire to retire at much earlier ages than average. For this group, an acceleration of the strategies discussed in this book may need to be employed.

Acknowledgments

I t is with much gratitude that I wish to thank the professionals who helped make this book possible.

Editor: Bobby Haas, Write On - Professional Editing Services, Thomas Locke

Publishing consultant: Polly Letofsky, My Word Publishing

Cover design: Virginia Wolf, Red Wolf Marketing

The grand essentials of happiness are
something to do, something to love,
and something to hope for.
—Allan K. Chalmers

Introduction

"Grandpa, what's retired?" asked the curly haired seven-year-old. Chuckling with nervous surprise, her grandfather responded, "Gosh, Casey, where did that question come from?"

There was silence as she pondered for a moment while they strolled toward their favorite neighborhood park. The late-morning sun cast their shadows on the sidewalk before them, which the grandfather watched with heartwarming gratitude as they walked along.

"Well, I asked Mommy why you always have time to play with me when other grown-ups are too busy, and she said because you are retired. Is retired your job?"

"Not exactly. These days my job is helping homeless animals find forever homes. I really enjoy doing that, and I still have lots of time to visit exciting places and do fun things like spend time with you."

"Daddy says he works hard so we can go on vacation to really fun places," said Casey. "Last year we spent two whole weeks at a beach house. That was fun! Is retirement a vacation, Grandpa?"

"Sort of. My vacations and playtimes are much longer than when I had a career, back when your mommy was a little girl like you. Now I get to choose when I work and when I play. It makes being your grandpa even more fun."

"Is retired just for grandparents?" Casey asked.

"You don't have to be a grandparent to be retired," he explained. "Most mommies and daddies work for a long, long time to save enough money to afford to be retired from their jobs so they can work and play when they choose. By that time, their children are grown, and they have their own families, but not always. When grown-ups can afford to do fun things with their time depends on how soon they finish all their homework."

"How did you know what homework you needed to do, Grandpa?"

"Well, I have a very special teacher who taught me what to do and gave me homework assignments to complete along the way. She helped me with the math and other important things I needed to know before I could spend more time playing rather than working. In fact, she is still helping me learn new things. She is a most important teacher to me."

"That sounds like my school, Grandpa. I like learning new things like science and math. My teacher and her helper, Miss Anne, say we can't go to recess and play until our homework is finished. Maybe retired is . . . recess, but for grown-ups."

With a loud laugh and a playful wink of his eye he answered, "Yes! That's right, Casey. Retirement is recess for grown-ups. Now let's play!"

Retirement Is Recess for Grown-Ups. When the Recess Bell Rings, Will You Be Ready?

I hate to put pressure on you—but the clock is ticking. Retirement is and has always been about time. For those who seize it, time provides opportunity during working years to capture a percentage of wages and deposit them into retirement savings accounts or other future income endeavors where the money compounds and grows toward a most important goal—financial independence. Squander time before saving begins, and a much higher contribution amount must be made to obtain the same financial goal. The greater amount is the cost of waiting to begin—the longer you wait, the higher the cost.

For those who do participate in their own financial destiny, contributory retirement accounts such as IRAs, 401(k) plans, and annuities are rapidly replacing the disappearing pension plans enjoyed for so many years by past generations. When funded, these new-era pension replacements are designed to supplement other retirement-income sources so that, together, they support a future lifestyle through which continuing to work may be optional, but living the dream you worked so many years to experience is not. As retirement dreams eventually awaken to become retirement reality, time and money resources must be managed diligently to ensure that financial independence lasts as long as you do—which, if current trends continue, could be a very long time!

In the past, becoming retired automatically commenced for most folks after reaching a certain age (typically sixty-five) and vesting enough time (usually an entire career with one company) to reach the golden status of "retired person." This achievement was often recognized with a retirement party and a gold watch presented in front of fellow work associates, a group of colleagues who dreamed of (or dreaded) their own inevitable bon voyage. Incidentally, the tradition of giving gold watches first originated back in the 1940s with PepsiCo. It was a heartfelt expression of gratitude: "You put in your time with us; now we are gifting you ours in the form of this watch." Originally, the retirement watches were 18-karat gold. In later years, they became gold-plated to save on costs. Nowadays, very few companies give watches to retiring employees; similar to company pensions, they are considered "not cost effective."

Today's current and future retirees are replacing the outdated gold watch of the past with a new symbol to commemorate this amazing lifetime achievement—"obtaining financial freedom before becoming too old to enjoy it." During grade school years, a recess bell is used to signal a highly anticipated break from the work of the classroom. Recess—it's a timeless tradition when kids exercise their legs and imaginations as they run and play, socialize, explore, climb a tree, or just hang out with friends. Isn't the spirit of these activities the type you wish to enjoy during what is traditionally called your retirement years? You know, take a well-deserved periodic or permanent break

from work and exercise your legs and imagination, run, play, socialize, explore, maybe climb a tree (or mountain), or just hang out with
friends? If so, let's replace the mundane ticking of the retirement gold
watch with the joyful ringing of a bell—the recess bell. Its ring is your
invitation to join a growing number of people who are trading in the
traditional status description of "I'm retired" and replacing it with a
new and enthusiastic declaration: *"I'm not retired; I'm at recess."*

A financially successful retirement is no longer an automatic rite
of passage. It's all up to you. Passive retirement hopefuls will need to
become active participants in their own financial futures if they wish
to re-create their lives to include the freedoms enjoyed by the financially well prepared: doing what they want, whenever they want, for as
long as they want. Even with a growing mountain of evidence to the
contrary, many people continue to act as if their plan to financial independence is somehow vesting automatically on its own, with no effort
required on their parts. No one—not the federal government and not
your employer—is secretly putting money in a GoFundMe account to
pay for your retirement. The days where all you need to do is show up
and collect are over.

Adequate preparation, including engaging in the process of comprehensive financial planning, will be the difference between experiencing a retirement lifestyle of your design or becoming dependent on
someone else's vision for your future—that being the person or institu-
tion whom you will depend on when you run out of money before you
run out of lifetime. Of course, creating a financial plan and failing to
take the necessary actions it identifies negates the entire purpose of
the plan.

Frequently absent from retirement preparation activities is the life-
planning exercise of deciding how you will spend not just money but
your time during retirement, a period that could last longer than all the

years you worked for a living. It seems odd that those who pay so much attention to exploring financial and money-management strategies often neglect to consider what they want to be, do, and have in retirement aside from simply being "retired," doing "activities," and having a "certain amount of money." Perhaps this occurs because, in the past, people were conditioned to expect and plan for shorter, more-predictable retirements. Simply stating you're going to "golf," "lay on the beach," "travel," or "pursue a hobby" are great examples of retirement activities, but they are just that—activities. Today's multidecade retirement lifestyles are made up of several facets in addition to enjoying your favorite pleasures. For example, contemporary retirement-life goals often include aspirations of "rehirement," where new employment opportunities are sought as a means to pay an invaluable career experience forward rather than reaping the benefits of that experience through a higher salary. Others seek entirely new vocational experiences in retirement that they didn't have the opportunity or financial ability to pursue during their primary careers. I know of a newly retired couple that opened a floral shop after lifetime careers working as aerospace engineers. They're not retired; they're at recess!

A side effect when anticipating a longer lifetime (longer-gevity) is an increased worrying about personal identity—not personal identity theft so much as personal identity meaning. Casting off familiar identities and trying on new life roles never worn before can feel intimidating and may hinder, even stall, progress toward securing the retirement life you are working so hard to achieve. Some new retirees, who have accumulated more than enough money to retire securely, may lack the confidence to ring the retirement-recess bell until they fully answer this important question: Who will I be during this new phase of life now that I'm no longer doing what I used to do for a living? Included in this book is an exercise designed to help you discover your retirement identity—not just in one or two, but in seven facets of your retirement lifestyle. I call this exercise *You Vision*. Readers are encouraged to complete this revealing homework regardless of age or the number of years before or after beginning retirement. Your answers may surprise you.

Once *You Vision* is completed, a financial plan can be crafted to answer important questions about investment and income-distribution strategies to fully fund it. Also, an assortment of financial, economic, and personal risks that may threaten an earlier-than-planned spend down of assets in retirement need to be assessed and mitigated by creating a retirement risk assessment.

Often, risk-mitigation strategies are limited in scope to investment management or utilizing insurance programs to reduce the financial impact if a specific risk event occurs. In addition to these areas, we will widen the risk-management discussion to include an assessment of additional threats to retirement income—these are known as "retirement income security killers" or RISK as an acronym. Creating an individual RISK assessment as an initial step in the financial planning process allows for early identification of any potential high-impact risks that can be addressed as the financial plan is crafted. This vital step will help ensure that the retirement financial plan you are creating will effectively address each of these risks sufficiently. Similar to personal health care, early detection screening and treatment of retirement income security killers before they become problematic is essential to safeguarding good retirement financial health at any age. Because risks are migratory in nature, meaning they can change as you do, an annual RISK assessment checkup is always prudent. When it comes to retirement preparation, what you don't know *can* hurt you.

Beyond the necessary life planning, money dynamics, and risk-assessment exercises required for today's retirement hopefuls, an honest self-appraisal of your capabilities, in the event you choose to act as your own financial adviser now and throughout all your retirement years, requires your careful evaluation. What begins early in working careers as a relatively simple financial plan consisting of establishing a cash reserve, managing debts, and contributing to a retirement account grows more complex as life stages progress. If you have already engaged the services of a competent retirement financial adviser, congratulations. She or he may have even given you this book as a pledge to provide ongoing retirement planning education for you. In addition, offering to personally help you complete the retirement-readiness homework exercises included in the chapters that follow is a testament to the highest professional standard shared only by elite retirement financial advisers.

Recent research reveals that six of ten people surveyed believe they are fully qualified to function as their own retirement financial adviser. However, upon closer examination, only two in ten actually possess sufficient time, knowledge, and emotional discipline to truly qualify as financially competent to advise themselves consistently over the long haul. Essential to your long-term success is an honest assessment of your current financial knowledge and retirement-planning capabilities. Ask yourself: Do I have enough "T"? No, not testosterone. But rather, do I have the retirement-planning hormones of time, training, and temperament to effectively be my own retirement financial adviser, not just today, but for the years in between now and my retirement age? And for all the decades that follow? Before you answer, keep in mind that retirement is a journey you have not taken before—a journey with few, if any, financial do-overs once your trip begins.

Within the large population of workers and retirees, there are those who are truly qualified to be their own financial adviser, those who know they aren't, and others who believe they are, but in reality, they aren't. Because I don't know you personally, I have no objective basis to decide which description most closely describes your actual financial aptitude. I have, however, included information in the chapters that follow to help you more accurately evaluate and answer the three-T questions for yourself.

Be assured, this book is not a disguise for an infomercial promoting me, my company, or anyone I know to become your financial savior. As a thirty-two-year, battle-hardened retirement financial adviser (retired), my purpose as author is to share my long-time professional experience with you, dispel myths, and provide practical, plain-English explanations regarding the recommended financial planning homework assignments required of those who seek the coveted status of "retirement-recess ready." For those who decide to pursue additional information about engaging professional financial planning help, chapter 14, Hiring a Lifetime Financial Adviser, is devoted to outlining proven ways to properly locate, vet, and hire the best of the best in financial retirement planning.

Throughout the pages that follow, you'll find retirement planning homework assignments. These are the recommended and often-necessary exercises that will better prepare you emotionally and financially for the retirement-recess lifestyle you envision. In addition to this textbook, I recommend you obtain the *Retirement Recess Homework/ Exercise Workbook*. I created this guide to help you more easily complete your retirement-planning homework assignments. The homework workbook is provided free for those who have purchased this book and can be downloaded at this website: www.retirementrecess.com.

You will also find *take note* statements as you read. Each note contains key points summarizing an important fact or trend or thought. These are like the CliffsNotes format you remember from your school years.

Finally, you will notice *extra credit* assignment icons inviting you to visit the retire-ready resource center at www.retirementrecess.com/retire-ready-resource-center. There you will find additional information regarding selected topics for those who wish to deepen their knowledge about important aspects of retirement planning. I will continue to expand and update this knowledge library, so check back often for updates.

It is my sincere hope that as you read *Retirement Is Recess for Grown-Ups,* you will do the following:

- **Inspire** and encourage the student inside you to always be open to learn new things. Knowledge provides power to change the things you can.
- **Perspire** as you sweat the risks that can threaten your financial well-being and learn how to identify and mitigate them before and not after they impact your financial security and retirement-recess playtime.
- **Conspire**, if applicable, to locate, interview, and hire a retirement planning professional who meets the ideals of a lifetime financial adviser described within.
- **Retire** on your terms and on your time. Gold watch optional!

Thank you for reading and best wishes for an amazing retirement-recess experience. I hope to see you on the playground real soon!

To further the efforts of early financial planning education in our high schools and colleges, a portion of the proceeds from the sale of this book are donated to not-for-profit organizations dedicated to improving financial literacy and retirement readiness of future generations of retirement-recess hopefuls. Contact the author at: jim@retirementrecess.com for more information.

Chapter One

The Evolution of Retirement—
How We Got to Where We Are

It's the early 1900s, and the plan for life is simple. You are born, live a short childhood, work, and die. Life expectancy is approximately forty-five years from cradle to grave. Imagine being considered really old while in your midforties by anyone other than your children!

The US economy is primarily agricultural and industrial sweat-labor-based. Many working men and women die on the farm field or the factory floor long before taking their ease in retirement. Consequently, there is little discussion about retirement planning around the kitchen table. For the majority of working folks, the idea of retirement simply doesn't exist. Those who live beyond their productive working years finish out their days in the assisted-living centers of the era—the private homes of family or friends who provide care and support for them as they close out the final chapters of their lives. On average, 75 percent of the people in the United States die before they reach age sixty-five in the early 1900s; compare that to a hundred years later (2010), when approximately 75 percent live beyond age sixty-five.

In the aftermath of the Great Depression of the 1930s, the lucky ones who keep their jobs tend to be senior in tenure and age. Unemployment remains highest among younger, able-bodied Americans unable to inherit the jobs of older workers who simply will not leave their posts. To provide an incentive to retire at age sixty-five (a few years older than the average life expectancy age during this period) with social dignity rather than working on, Social Security retirement benefits are introduced in 1935. Social Security provides a monetary incentive for seniors to retire while allowing younger, underemployed workers to fill the vacated jobs.

TAKE NOTE

ON AVERAGE, 75 PERCENT OF THE PEOPLE IN THE UNITED STATES DIED BEFORE THEY REACHED AGE SIXTY-FIVE IN THE EARLY 1900S COMPARED TO A HUNDRED YEARS LATER (2010), WHEN APPROXIMATELY 75 PERCENT LIVED BEYOND AGE SIXTY-FIVE.

THE 1950S—HAPPY DAYS

Thanks in large part to improved working conditions, average life expectancy has improved significantly since the early 1900s. At age sixty-five, retirement income you can't outlive is provided by Social Security along with public or private funded pensions for those who are eligible to receive them. These two primary retirement-income sources further reinforce age sixty-five as the "full-benefit retirement age" for most working Americans. Once a retiree begins receiving either of these two income entitlements, that person is paid out monthly benefits for a lifetime. In other words, regardless of how long you live, pension and Social Security checks, like the rock and roll hits of this era, just keep on coming. This period in history becomes known as the *golden era* of retirement entitlement income.

Retirees living during the golden era (recent survivors of the Great Depression period) use cash savings rather than credit for major purchases and most often are home-mortgage free by their retirement ages. Some newly retired folks organize neighborhood block parties where they celebrate mortgage debt independence day by burning their mortgage loan documents after their last house payment is made. "Layaway" (the opposite of revolving consumer credit) is utilized as a purchase strategy for consumer goods, allowing an item to be bought and paid for over a period of months before taking possession of it after the final payment is made. I remember my mother going to a local department store each month to make an installment payment on a dress it was holding for her until the final payment was received. During each visit, the store clerk would go to a back room and bring out the laid-away dress for her to see. She would smile and reply "only a few more payments, and I'll be able to wear it home."

In future years, easy credit will seduce consumers into enjoying a "have it now, pay for it later" retail credit mentality. For the overextended grown kids of the World War II generation parents, layaway will become "lay awake" in financial fear as "later" arrives sooner than the financial means to pay for the financed item. Many Generation X and Y kids of the baby boomers will also carry huge student loan debt along with them to job interviews, hoping that if hired, they will be able to retire their college debt before they reach their own retirement age.

For retirees living during the golden era, supplemental savings and investments provide money for nonessential expenses such as travel and extras while guaranteed-income entitlements pay for basic essential expenses, providing a relatively stable and predictable source of income for most retired folks.

THE 1990S, RETIRE EARLY, PARTY ON

In the decade of the 1990's many early retirees locked in lower, permanent lifetime-income benefits from Social Security and pensions. Consequently, the demand for early pension payouts over longer life-expectancy periods begins to escalate the cost for employers who fund private and public pension plans. In response, companies and organizations begin to curtail their future pension programs for those who are still working, and in some cases, they reduce pension-income benefits for existing retirees. As a growing number of retirees claim reduced income payments from Social Security and pensions at younger-than-full-retirement ages, they begin to rely more heavily on overvalued retirement investment accounts to fill the gap between a rising cost of living and reduced entitlement income amounts. A booming economy during the go-go eighties and nineties, soaring real estate values, and record gains in the stock market give people a greater sense of financial confidence. Some make the shortsighted mistake of believing that overvalued investment returns from retirement accounts earned over the past two decades (1980s–1990s) are permanent and will continue in the future without any periodic value pullbacks along the way. In believing so, many request excess income distributions absent a more cautious income drawdown strategy from their bloated investment accounts. After all, what's the worst thing that could happen?

FROM BOOM TO BUST

There was a sense the economic boom party of the 1980s and '90s was ending, especially for those relying heavily on overvalued stock for retirement income. In December of 1996 the then-chairman of the Federal Reserve, Alan Greenspan, described the huge run-up in the US stock market with the words "irrational exuberance." It took several years from the date of Greenspan's observation, but what followed created a lot of irrational behavior and was anything but exuberant. If the 1920s were roaring, the 1990s were soaring. Both of these infamous decades were followed with huge financial and economic shocks—the Great Depression of the 1930s and the early 2000s recession in 2002 and 2003. That was followed by the Great Recession of 2007 to 2009.

So the first decade of the new millennium brought not one but two epic setback periods. Both historic economic periods of decline would later be followed by recovery. But that was not to be for millions of retirees witnessing their retirement investments becoming permanently decimated as the result of panic selling or because they requested excess distributions during these epic financial downturns.

To make matters worse, by the late 2000s, record low interest rates (artificially depressed by the Federal Reserve to help stabilize the weak economy after the 2008 home mortgage meltdown) all but eliminated the ability for retirees to receive ample traditional guaranteed interest income from sources such as bank CDs, bonds, and insurance annuity programs.

Also contributing to retirement-planning difficulties were soaring retirement health-care costs (both insurance premiums and out-of-pocket expenses). Escalating insurance premiums became unaffordable for many early retirement hopefuls who were younger than the Medicare eligibility age of sixty-five. The Affordable Health Care Act

(ACA) (Obamacare), passed into law in 2010, was our country's most recent major health-care insurance overhaul; it attempted to curtail increasing health-care insurance costs while making health insurance available to everyone regardless of current health and age. Although twenty-three million people who previously were uninsurable were able to receive health insurance as a result of the ACA, premiums and out-of-pocket deductibles continued to rise for the masses. As of this writing (2018), no national health insurance replacement plan to fix the ACA had been successfully passed into law by Congress.

EXTRA CREDIT

GO TO WWW.RETIREMENTRECESS.COM/RETIRE-READY-RESOURCE-CENTER FOR UPDATES AND THE LATEST INFORMATION ON RETIREMENT HEALTH AND HEALTH-CARE INSURANCE TRENDS.

RETIREMENT AGE INCREASES

Due to increasing longevity, lack of financial preparation, and major economic, financial, and political shifts, the retirement age of the workforce is steadily increasing. A 2015 Employee Benefit Research Institute (EBRI) Retirement Confidence Survey reported that 16 percent of workers said the age at which they expected to retire had changed in the past year. Eighty-one percent of this group reported that the age they planned to retire had increased.

It's important to note that when preretirees are asked about their anticipated retirement age, there is often a difference between the age they *plan* to retire and the *actual* age that retirement begins. Younger workers are generally more optimistic (and possibly naive) about their financial futures and will often claim they plan to retire at an earlier age. As time passes and they realize they are not fully financially and emotionally ready, they push their retirement age out, hoping outside forces such as their health and employment demand agree with their age extension. Recent studies show that as many as four in ten workers (40 percent) actually retire earlier than planned due to unexpected changes in their health, the health of a family member, or changes in their work environment. Due to circumstances beyond their control, these early retirees are not always financially prepared to take a permanent leave from their employers.

For those who have chosen to continue to work beyond the traditional retirement age of sixty-five, working longer can provide the benefit of additional time to finish necessary financial homework assignments discussed in this book. But the decision to work longer to improve retirement readiness doesn't occur without increasing other risks, such as employment risk. Simply stated, employment risk is the increasing probability of becoming unemployable due to a health condition or an adverse employment trend, regardless of the intent to work on. When employment ends, so does employment income.

It is essential for those who continue to work past traditional retirement ages to create a contingent retirement-income plan (investments, rental income, spousal income) that will become available when primary employment income stops.

TAKE NOTE

THE LACK OF ADEQUATE RETIREMENT PREPARATION IS THE PRIMARY REASON WHY THE AVERAGE RETIREMENT AGE WILL CONTINUE TO RISE IN THE FUTURE.

BACK TO THE FUTURE—EXTENDED LIFE EXPECTANCY

Approximately one out of every four sixty-five-year-olds living in the first decade of the new millennium will continue to do so past age ninety. Couples have increased odds of one of the pair living past age ninety-five, based on recent research by the Social Security Administration. Healthier living habits, improved sanitation, and advances in technology and medicine all team up to eradicate many of the diseases of past generations that proved fatal at younger ages, such as polio, small pox, and tuberculosis. Remaining to still be cured are the diseases that kill us more slowly as we age, such as Alzheimer's and Parkinson's. These long-term diseases create additional challenges to an already-complex financial planning process. Retirement hopefuls not only need to find the extra money from already-tight budgets to save for their retirement, but they also need to determine ways to make it last much longer than previous generations.

Research on aging concludes that increases in longevity are showing no signs of tapering off soon, even for those at the far end of the age spectrum. In 2014, the number of Americans age one hundred-plus was over 72,000, up 44 percent since the year 2000. Not only are there more people than ever blowing out one hundred candles on their cakes, but also they themselves as a group are living even longer past the milestone age of one hundred. Death rates declined for all demographic groups of centenarians in the six years ending in 2014, according to the Centers for Disease Control and Prevention. It should come as no surprise that women continue to lead men in the longevity race.

Chapter Two

The Retirement-Income Stool

The three traditional retirement-income sources relied upon by past generations—Social Security, company pensions, and personal savings and investments—are referred to as legs on the three-legged retirement-income stool. For decades, the image of this stool symbolized these three unwavering sources of retirement income that, when equally distributed, funded a balanced, stable plan for retirement living.

DON'T SIT ON THAT STOOL; THE LEGS ARE BROKEN!

Today, that stool is extremely unstable. The Social Security leg is cracked, the pension leg is disappearing, and the retirement savings leg is way too thin to bear the weight of those future retirees who sit upon it for what could be a thirty- to forty-year retirement period.

THE CRACKED SOCIAL SECURITY-INCOME LEG

In 1935 the Social Security retirement-benefit program was established, defining age sixty-five as the full retirement age. At the time of enactment, it was widely believed and supported by life expectancy data that most workers who paid into the Social Security system during their working years and retired at age sixty-five would not live long after. Consequently, the Social Security system would remain actuarially sound due to payroll taxes paid by a younger, growing workforce that would far exceed benefits paid out to those living relatively short retirement lives.

The very first Social Security payee was a fellow named Ernest Ackerman, who got a payment of seventeen cents in January 1937. This was a one-time, lump-sum payout, which was the only form of benefits paid during the start-up period of January 1937 through December 1939.

Ida Wins the Government Lottery

Ida May Fuller (Aunt Ida) was the first beneficiary of recurring monthly Social Security payments. Thus, Social Security check number 00-000-001, dated January 31, 1940, was issued to Ida May Fuller in the amount of $22.54. Having paid into Social Security for just three years, she received monthly Social Security checks until her death in 1975 at age—wait for it—one hundred. By the time of her passing, Ida had collected $22,888.92 in Social Security benefits—compared to her total contribution of $24.75 into the system. Uncle Sam was very generous to Aunt Ida.

Although Ms. Fuller's long lifetime was an anomaly at the time, her long life beyond age sixty-five was an augury for what the Social Security system is experiencing today in much greater frequency—a record number of retired workers collecting Social Security over much longer life spans than originally envisioned. Even so, Congress has only enacted one age adjustment to Social Security retirement benefits since 1935. The 1983 Social Security Amendment included a provision to raise the full retirement age for citizens born in 1938 or later, gradually increasing the full retirement age to sixty-seven for people born after 1959.

Other benefit changes to Social Security over the years include the following:

- **Widening the net of eligibility.** Under the original 1935 law, Social Security only paid retirement benefits to the primary worker. A 1939 change in the law added survivors benefits for the retiree's spouse and children. In 1956, disability benefits were added.
- **Adding annual cost-of-living adjustments to benefit amounts.** Cost-of-living adjustments (COLAs) were first paid in 1975 as a result of a 1972 law. Prior to this, benefits were increased irregularly by special acts of Congress.

Social Security Payroll Taxes Past and Present

The Social Security Act of 1935 set the initial tax rate at 2 percent (employee and employer combined) on a maximum of $3,000 of taxable income, and it mandated specified increases that would bring this rate to 6 percent by 1949.

The law went on to say, "Beginning in 1949, twelve years from now, you and your employer will each pay three cents on every dollar you earn [3 percent], up to $3,000 of income a year. That is the most you will ever pay." But it was a broken promise. As of 2019, the maximum payroll tax collected per person has grown to 12.4 percent (the employer pays 6.2 percent, and the employee pays 6.2 percent), paid on income earned up to $132,900.

For retirement-planning purposes, expect additional Social Security tax increases to continue in the future. Part of "fixing" the actuarially broken Social Security system will involve raising taxes on workers and employers. Some studies conclude that an estimated 2.5 percent increase in the payroll tax shared by employees and employers each will be needed to fix the underfunding problem. The questions that remain are these: When will this increase occur? What will it be called for political purposes? How much will it be? Who will pay it?

It doesn't matter what Congress calls it, whether it be The Future Generations Security Act, or The Better Now Than Later Act, it is still going to be a tax increase. Plan on it, and plan for it!

Who Is Relying on Social Security Retirement-Income Benefits?

A reminder from the Social Security Administration: "Social Security was never meant to be the only source of income for people when they retire." Remember the original retirement-income stool? Three income legs, not one. Despite the original intention of Social Security benefits, individuals age sixty-five and older who receive those benefits report the following:

- For 52 percent of married couples and 74 percent of unmarried persons, 50 percent or more of their income is derived from Social Security.
- Approximately 22 percent of married couples and about 47 percent of unmarried persons rely on Social Security for 90 percent or more of their household income.

TAKE NOTE

THE US BUREAU OF THE CENSUS SURVEY FOUND THAT RECIPIENTS IN 2015 RELIED ON SOCIAL SECURITY BENEFITS TO REPLACE NEARLY 41 PERCENT OF PRERETIREMENT INCOME COMPARED WITH 23 PERCENT IN 1940.

"Third Rail" Syndrome

Although Social Security income is and will continue to be an important retirement-income source for future generations, the system's projected growing shortfall is the subject of increasing speculation and worry. Even though some politicians stoop so low as to fabricate false Social Security scare stories and use them against their opponents in elections, most politicians are hesitant to "reform" (political-speak for higher taxes/fewer benefits) the system for fear of constituent retaliation at the voting booth.

Former US House Speaker Thomas "Tip" O'Neill referred to Social Security as the "third rail of American politics." The third rail in the middle of a subway track carries high voltage to power the train—touch it and you're dead. Politicians and reformers have long negative experience with the backlash from voters when proposing or even talking out loud about changes to "fix" the system that everyone desperately needs and agrees is broken and in need of repair. Since the only way to repair the system is to raise taxes and/or cut benefits, nobody wants to be the first to touch this politically charged rail by proposing changes to fix Social Security.

I Hear the Train A Comin'

Perhaps the irony of the hands-off, touch-it–and-politically-die Washington policy is that the time is fast approaching when it will be political suicide for elected officials to *not* put forth and pass responsible reforms. There soon will be increased political pressure on both sides of the aisle to mend this broken entitlement program before it becomes truly too late to fix. It is a bipartisan actuarial problem.

In the 2018 Annual Report to Congress, the Social Security trustees announced this: "The asset reserves of the combined OASDI Trust Funds increased by $44 billion in 2017 to a total of $2.89 trillion. The total annual cost of the program is projected to exceed total annual income in 2018 for the first time since 1982, and remain higher throughout the 75-year projection period. As a result, asset reserves are expected to decline during 2018."

If no changes are enacted, the asset reserves of the Social Security trust fund are projected to become depleted in 2034, with only 77 percent of full benefits payable after that date from continuing payroll taxes. Beginning in 2035, Social Security recipients would experience a reduction of twenty-three cents on each dollar of benefit they received. Although no one except those who prey on the fears of voters for political reasons believes our government will allow this to happen, we may have to wait a while to find out. As you know, Congress is famous for eleventh-hour fixes.

A Reserve with No Actual Cash in It

Where is the 2.89 trillion-dollar Social Security trust fund cash kept? Fort Knox? A bank account in Switzerland? The National Archives? The answer is this: None of the above. By law, as Social Security taxes are collected, excess Social Security payroll tax revenues beyond current expenditures (benefits) are spent by Congress for other things. In their place, an IOU is issued in the form of a Treasury bond. There is not now nor has there ever been an actual "lockbox" stuffed with billions of cash reserves, as some politicians have implied over the years. Ironically, Congress has recently introduced a bill called "The Social Security Lockbox Act" to limit future IOU spending practices of excess Social Security reserves. Since Social Security excess reserves have been spent for decades and future surpluses are ending in 2018, there is little doubt any congressional measure to safeguard reserves will be too late in arriving.

Want to have some fun? Ask the congressional representative for your district or state where the Social Security trust fund reserve is located? Send the responses to me so I can post them on our website for others to read.

We are fast approaching a period when changes will need to be implemented—aka politically touching the third rail—before the cost of this eighty-year shell game is just too high to manage.

No matter how Washington spins reform, any real change will require a policy of "more or less." "More" will probably mean a defined group of taxpayers (most likely higher-income earners) paying *more* payroll or benefit taxes. "Less" will probably mean a group of targeted benefit recipients (most likely younger workers) receiving fewer benefits either by extending the retirement age when benefits can be received, cutting future income benefits to certain groups, or both.

Social Security reform ideas currently being considered include the following:

- **Linking the cost-of-living adjustment (COLA) to an index other than the consumer price index (CPI).** Social Security benefits are adjusted each year to keep up with inflation as measured by the consumer price index for urban wage earners and clerical workers (CPI-W). A different measure of inflation could be used that typically grows more slowly than CPI-W. If used, that measure would save the system money while depriving the recipient of the ability to stay current with real-life cost-of-living increases.

- **Phased-in increases in the Social Security tax rate.** Gradually increase the percentage of tax owed by both employees and employers from 6.2 percent (each) on the first $132,900 (2019) of taxable earnings to a higher percentage (possibly a 2.5 percent increase) and/or increase the taxable wage base to a higher amount.

- **Raising the retirement benefit age.** Social Security's full-benefit retirement age is sixty-six-plus for those born prior to 1960 and age sixty-seven for everyone born later. Benefit payments are reduced if you sign up and receive Social Security income before your full retirement age. Amounts are higher if you wait until age seventy to draw benefits. One proposed idea is gradually raising the full-retirement age from sixty-seven to sixty-eight between the years 2023 and 2028 for those born later than 1960. This change would reduce benefits by about 7 percent and decrease Social Security's financial shortfall by 16 percent.

- **Means testing.** Means testing Social Security would reduce or eliminate retirement payments for retirees at higher income levels. This idea was acceptance-tested (polled) several years ago under the false belief that the wealthy wouldn't mind giving up part or all of their benefits. The response? Wrong! A resounding "Yes, I am expecting a payback for what I paid in" was the message returned to Congress, regardless of personal net-worth.

Although it is widely believed that any future reforms to Social Security will most likely affect younger workers who have time to adjust, all reform ideas carry the risk of impacting everyone in some way.

> **TAKE NOTE**
>
> TO REDUCE YOUR SOCIAL SECURITY ENTITLEMENT RISK, TAKE STEPS NOW TO BECOME LESS DEPENDENT ON SOCIAL SECURITY BENEFITS DURING YOUR FUTURE RETIREMENT YEARS. IN OTHER WORDS, SAVE MORE AND DEPEND ON OTHERS, INCLUDING THE GOVERNMENT, LESS.

THE DISAPPEARING PENSION LEG

Prior to the 1870s, private-sector pension plans did not exist in the US, primarily because most companies were small, family-run enterprises.

In 1875 the American Express Company became the first major corporation to offer a private pension plan. Banks and manufacturing companies followed soon after and began offering employees company-sponsored pension plans to recruit and retain employment talent.

During World War II, the federal government froze wages for a time in an attempt to curb wartime inflation. To attract employees in a tight labor market (since so many workers were employed by the military), private employers began offering increasingly generous pension plans as a lure to work for their companies. Their message was clear: "We know our wages are low now, but come work for us, and we promise a great lifetime-guaranteed retirement-income benefit later—a retirement pension you can't outlive."

From 1940 to 1960, the number of people enrolled in company-sponsored pension plans ballooned from about 3.7 million to over 23 million, covering nearly 30 percent of the full-time workforce. At its peak in the 1980s, 38 million workers (38 percent of all workers) were covered through 180,000 plans, according to a survey titled *Employee Benefits in Industry* conducted by the Bureau of Labor Statistics.

Pension Extinction

By 2005, there were fewer than 80,000 qualified pension plans. As of 2011, only 10 percent of private employers offered pension plans, accounting for only 18 percent of the private workforce. What happened? The primary reasons pensions have become and are continuing to become extinct are similar to the reasons why Social Security benefits are at risk of becoming an endangered species:

- Increasing costs to maintain pensions hamper the ability of companies to fund a growing future liability that will require benefits to be paid to retired workers for longer periods than originally projected.
- Fewer workers contributing to a company's pension pool support a large number of recipients who are drawing lifetime benefits over an extended period of time.
- Unique to pension plans are funding regulations imposed by the federal or state government, and those regulations have increased to the point where maintaining a pension is cost prohibitive for most corporations.

Other issues affecting pension plan viability are historically low interest rates and an underperforming stock market, especially during the first decade of the new millennium. All of these factors have increased pressure on pension managers to seek higher investment returns to meet higher funding requirements by assuming greater risk.

Today, many pension plans are in the red or dead. More than two-thirds of the companies that make up the S&P 500 have defined-benefit plans on their books, and at the end of 2013, only eighteen of them were fully funded. Estimates of underfunded corporate pensions in the S&P 500 top $557 billion, according to the consulting firm Mercer. This increasing unpaid tab is especially of concern for both those who are receiving pension benefits and those who are vested but not yet receiving benefits.

Pension Guarantee

The Pension Benefit Guaranty Corporation (PBGC) was created by the Employee Retirement Income Security Act of 1974 (ERISA) to encourage the continuation and maintenance of voluntary private defined-benefit pension plans. The PBGC insurance program pays pension benefits up to the maximum single life guaranteed benefit to participants who retire at sixty-five ($64,432 in 2017).

According to Wikipedia, in fiscal year 2015, PBGC paid $5.6 billion in benefits to participants of failed single-employer pension plans (one employer paying many pension participants). That year, sixty-nine single-employer pension plans failed. PBGC paid $103 million in financial assistance to fifty-seven multiemployer pension plans (multiple employers paying benefits to many pension participants). The agency's deficit increased by $76 billion overall. It has a total of $164 billion in obligations and $88 billion in assets. This is not a healthy balance sheet for pension recipients.

Pension Buyout

Because of corporate pension funding pressures, many companies are offering vested pension participants a buyout option. This is an offer by the employer pension plan custodian to pay out a lump-sum amount to the participant now in lieu of pension income payments for life. If offered as a qualified lump-sum payout, the amount can be rolled over tax-free to an IRA account by the recipient. Although the Steve Miller Band sang, "Take the money and run" in the 1970s, careful consideration should be given to any pension lump-sum offer. Financial advisers recommend the recipient calculate the current value of future pension payments and compare this value with the current pension buyout offer. If you have no clue about what I just wrote, consider hiring a financial pro by the hour to assist you with this very important decision. Bottom line: You need to determine what is best for you both now and in the future before making what could be an irreversible decision. Other considerations might include how you, the former employee, feel about the future solvency of the company sponsoring the pension. Also, consider how you feel about what you just learned about the financial solvency of the Pension Benefit Guarantee Corporation. And think about how confident you are about earning potentially higher investment returns on the buyout money by investing and assuming any future risk yourself once the pension buyout amount is deposited in your IRA. In other words, do you believe you can outperform the pension fund over time?

Major Transition of Retirement Funding Responsibility— Investing Versus Vesting for Retirement Income

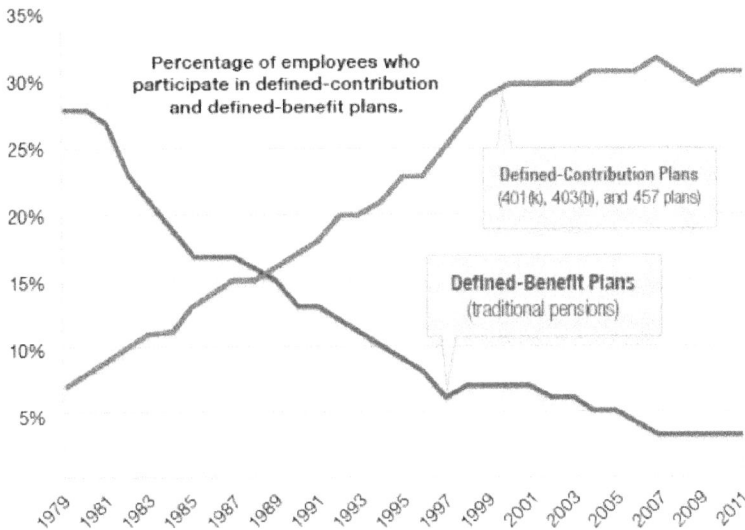

Percentage of employees who participate in defined-contribution and defined-benefit plans.

Defined-Contribution Plans (401(k), 403(b), and 457 plans)

Defined-Benefit Plans (traditional pensions)

Source: Bureau of Labor Statistics, 2013.
No survey data is available for 1992–1993, 2001–2002, and 2004.

Employer-paid company pension plans (defined-benefit plans), once a stable source of lifetime retirement income for over a third of workers and their spouses, are being rapidly replaced with employee-participation retirement plans called *defined-contribution plans*. The most common type is the 401(k) plan, named after the section of the Internal Revenue Code that made those plans possible by a law that was enacted in 1978. Defined-contribution retirement plans shift the responsibility and the cost for funding retirement income from the employer to the employee.

The traditional pension plan offers the recipient the security of having future income for life at a defined age—the maximum benefit usually begins at age sixty-five. This encourages the employee to retire only after achieving sufficient years of service and salary to have optimized the pension benefit. Some workers "put in their time" with employers until they reach their "optimum" benefit age and then retire. While still working, future pension recipients are able to forecast with certainty their lifetime retirement income from a pension at a given age, assuming, of course, that the pension payout rules for an employer plan do not change beforehand.

By contrast, when contributing to a defined-contribution plan such as a 401(k), a participant's actual retirement income at a given age is dependent on several variables:

- The amount of employee contributions.
- The employer-match contributions, if any.
- The actual investment performance resulting from investment selections.
- The date distributions are taken.
- Whether the recipient elected a lifetime income payout at retirement or not.

Due to these and other variables, many of which are unknown by the employee, most participants in 401(k) plans have no idea how much income they will receive from their plan in the future. This uncertainty is an unintentional incentive to continue to work beyond normal retirement ages.

EXTRA CREDIT

GO TO WWW.RETIREMENTRECESS.COM/RETIRE-READY-RESOURCE-CENTER AND SELECT "GETTING AN A IN 401(K)" TO LEARN MORE ABOUT MAXIMIZING YOUR COMPANY'S 401(K) RESULTS.

THE TOO-SHORT SAVINGS LEG OF THE RETIREMENT-INCOME STOOL

Party Like It's 1999—Save Like It's 1959

The current savings rate for future retirement hopefuls in qualified retirement plans or supplemental investment accounts is simply not enough for the vast majority of workers to meet current and future retirement-income demands—unless you're retiring in the 1950s. Even then it may be a stretch.

According to the Employee Benefit Research Institute's Twenty-Fourth Annual Retirement Confidence Survey, published in 2014, 65 percent of private-sector workers had access to a defined-contribution retirement plan (401(k)) through their employers. The fact that fewer than half of employees who were eligible to contribute actually participated in one is nothing short of alarming. An update of this statistic in 2016 shows no improvement—which is even more disturbing. Do we need to be grading on a curve here?

While an employer-sponsored retirement plan such as a 401(k) (the maximum contribution set for 2019 was $19,000) is a convenient and efficient way to save for retirement, the lack of such a plan is not an acceptable reason for failing to save for retirement—at least not with me. IRAs and Roth IRAs (for those eligible to contribute) are two great options available to anyone with earned income. The maximum annual contribution amount for either is $6,000 (in 2019) per participant with an additional $1,000 catch-up amount for those over the age of 50. Additionally, tax-deferred variable and fixed-rate annuity programs and tax-efficient asset allocation investment accounts all having no maximum contribution or income limitations are also available to anyone with discretionary income at any age.

The above-mentioned survey went on to show an increase from the previous report in respondents who are confident they will have enough money to last throughout their retirement (18 percent), but only 11 percent of the total respondents reported having $250,000 or more in their retirement accounts. A shocking 36 percent have less than $1,000 saved. This survey reveals a disconnect between the amount of actual retirement savings and what workers "confidently" believe is enough to finance a thirty-year retirement.

I remember my father thinking if he saved $50,000 between his IRA and a spousal IRA for my mother, they would have enough supplemental retirement savings for their lifetimes when they retired in 1986 at age sixty-two. Luckily, my parents were fortunate to have had several vested pensions provided by the state and military to supplement their savings to sustain them for their retirement lifetimes, which lasted more than thirty years. They also had lifetime medical insurance coverage provided by the military. At the time, $50,000 sounded like a lot of money to a working-class family, but in the context of being able to buy less each year due to inflation, it wasn't nearly enough without the added income from lifetime-guaranteed entitlements provided by Social Security and pensions. Fortunately, my parents had strong retirement-income legs on their retirement-income stool thanks to Social Security and pensions, and those two legs were able to compensate for the rather thin personal-savings leg.

An updated June 2015 Government Accountability Office analysis found that the average Americans between the ages of fifty-five and sixty-four have accrued about $104,000 in retirement savings. Sound like a lot? Not when you realize this sum buys approximately $560 in monthly income as a pension alternative if the money were invested in a guaranteed, non-inflation-protected lifetime annuity at age sixty-five.

Replacing a Pension

A saver may need to accumulate $500,000–$750,000 to replace an average lifetime pension payment in today's dollars. Some will argue this value needs to be higher or lower depending on circumstances. No matter how you calculate it, it's a huge amount of money. Remember, pension income was intended to replace about one-third of the total retirement-income need. With pension extinction, the difference is expected to come from Social Security (limited) and personal retirement savings.

Build It and They Will Come—or Not

As a society, we need to stop believing the federal government will magically rescue us from our national retirement savings crisis. After all, our government already has its own deficit dilemma to the tune of $20 trillion and growing. Additionally, don't believe the solution to our lack of retirement savings will be answered by adding more retirement savings account choices. Federal law has already established several retirement savings account programs that people of all ages and income ranges can utilize by just adding money. Personal retirement plans include IRA and Roth IRA. Employer-sponsored plans include these: 401(k), 401(a), 457, 403(b). The small-business, self-employed people have easy access to Simplified Employee Pension (SEP) IRAs, Keogh plans, Savings Incentive Match Plan for Employees (SIMPLE) IRAs, and single-employee (solo) 401(k) plans. All of these plans offer a wide range of investment choices, income tax benefits, and protection from lawsuits for participants. For more detailed information on any or all of the above-listed retirement account types, simply go to an internet financial search site such as Investopedia at http://www.investopedia.com for more information.

The problem isn't that the place to save for retirement doesn't exist; it's that people aren't adequately funding the retirement accounts currently available to them. As you learned in the extra credit "Getting an A in 401(k)," many participants who are contributing to employer-sponsored retirement savings accounts are not taking full advantage of employer-match contributions. It is still hard for me to fathom so many people refusing free money in the form of an employer 401(k) company match if they would only do what they needed to be doing all along—participating in their own financial future and contributing to their 401(k) accounts throughout their working careers.

EXTRA CREDIT

GO TO WWW.RETIREMENTRECESS.COM/RETIRE-READY-RESOURCE-CENTER AND STUDY CREATING THE MILLION DOLLAR RETIREMENT SAVINGS ACCOUNT—ONE DOLLAR AT A TIME.

Emergency Reserves Are NSF (Not Sufficiently Funded) for Most Savers

Redeeming money from your coveted retirement-savings investment plans (assuming you have one) for short-term cash emergencies prior to retirement will earn you an "F" grade in retirement-savings class. Not only are taxes and early withdrawal penalties assessed in many situations, but the loss of potential future income from the redeemed principal value can be extremely hard to replace over time. For most workers, getting the money saved initially is hard to accomplish; trying to replace the withdrawn amount while continuing to add new contributions toward your retirement-income goal can be next to impossible.

Some employer retirement savings plans (e.g. 401(k)) allow participants to borrow funds tax-and penalty-free from their retirement accounts and pay themselves back with interest over time. Even though this borrowing feature saves tax and possible early distribution penalties on the loan amount, it doesn't solve the cash flow problem of paying back the loan in addition to contributing what you normally need to be paying yourself for your future financial security. This whole 401(k) borrowing idea sounds a lot like the federal government's ongoing mismanagement of the Social Security trust fund we discussed earlier—borrowing and spending money that is earmarked specifically for your retirement future and worrying about the consequences and the huge costs to pay it back later.

To make a bad idea even worse, if a participant's loan balance is not paid back within sixty days of termination of employment, the amount is usually treated as a lump-sum taxable distribution. If the participant is under age fifty-nine and a half when employment ends, early tax penalties (10 percent) are assessed on unpaid loan balances. The result of paying both federal and state income taxes plus a 10 percent tax penalty could create a cost on the borrowed 401(k) account amount greater than 40 percent, depending on your other taxable income. If you are under age fifty-nine and a half and borrowed $5,000 for a down payment on a car from your 401(k) and did not repay the loan before leaving your employer, the cost of the loan could top $2,000! Doesn't your uncle Bennie lend money to family members at a cheaper cost?

> **TAKE NOTE**
>
> THE PARTICIPANT LOAN FEATURE OF A 401(K) RETIREMENT ACCOUNT SHOULD ONLY BE CONSIDERED AS A LAST, AND I MEAN VERY LAST, ALTERNATIVE.

A better strategy to cover the costs of the "life happens" kinds of expenses is a cash-emergency and short-term-goal account. The cost? Only the low interest you earn on the reserve, which is the price of liquidity. Because cash-reserve accounts are funded with after-tax money, the only tax you pay is on earnings, which I just disclosed are low. There are no tax-penalty costs and no requirement to pay the money back beyond your need to eventually replenish the reserve account before the next auto transmission (emergency) or beach chair (vacay).

Emergency expenses are best reserved in cash savings accounts or other reserve sources apart from your serious long-term-money retirement accounts. A common cash savings goal of three to six months of the monthly average of your essential expenses is often recommended. Your actual reserve goal amount may be adjusted from this rule-of-thumb amount based on your history of experiencing short-term financial emergencies and the nature of your near-term money goals.

Another source for ready cash reserves for short-term emergencies is a standby home equity line of credit if you are a homeowner with net equity (home value minus mortgage amount) in the property. Additionally, a no- or low-interest credit card can also be used for short-term expenses. Beware, these two options require cash repayments from income to pay back the loans and low/no-interest credit card offers usually morph into high-interest credit card rates after a specified time has elapsed.

TAKE NOTE

ESTABLISH AND MAINTAIN A PRUDENT CASH EMERGENCY FUND—USUALLY A SAVINGS ACCOUNT AT A BANK OR CREDIT UNION. ALSO, CONSIDER ONLINE, HIGH-YIELD SAVINGS ACCOUNTS THAT ARE LIQUID AND FDIC-INSURED BUT OFFERED BY NONBANK ENTITIES. CURRENT INTEREST RATES (AT ONE POINT IN 2018) ARE 2 PERCENT. USE THESE FUNDS RATHER THAN YOUR RETIREMENT SAVINGS TO COVER UNEXPECTED COSTS. OTHER SHORT-TERM CASH-RESERVE SOURCES INCLUDE A HOME EQUITY LINE OF CREDIT (ANY AGE) OR A REVERSE MORTGAGE LINE OF CREDIT FOR THOSE OVER AGE SIXTY-TWO WITH HOME EQUITY.

Chapter Three

Not Ready for Retirement Recess

Record numbers of baby boomers (ten thousand) are turning sixty-five every day (notice I didn't say "retiring") and will continue to do so for the next several years, except those still trapped in the 1960s! Yet many are not financially or emotionally prepared to graduate from the work-for-a-living class to the play-as-a-lifestyle retirement-recess group.

FANTASY MEETS REALITY—BUMMER!

For a growing number of baby boomers, particularly those who have not taken steps to plan and save accordingly, retirement reality is simply not aligning with retirement expectations. Essentially, the amount of retirement savings many boomers think or hope will be sufficient to fund an anticipated standard of retirement living is, quite simply, not enough.

According to a 2015 update on retirement preparedness conducted by the Insured Retirement Institute (IRI), there was a decline in overall retirement satisfaction among those already retired, plunging to 45 percent in 2015 from 72 percent in 2014. These results suggest there is widespread dissatisfaction developing among boomers as large numbers of them transition into their preretirement and retirement years. The Rolling Stones sang about this discontentment way back in 1966: "I Can't Get No Satisfaction." Of course, as of early 2018, the lead singer, Mick Jagger, was still working.

The study also revealed that only six in ten boomers report having money saved for retirement, down sharply from prior years, when approximately eight in ten had retirement savings. Of those who report having retirement savings, the percentage of boomers feeling extremely or very confident they will have enough money to last throughout retirement has declined significantly, to 27 percent in 2015 from almost 40 percent in 2011.

Boomers and the Gen Xers and Ys who don't successfully graduate from the working classroom to retirement recess are most likely unprepared due to one or more of the following reasons discussed below.

LACK OF RETIREMENT PLANNING KNOWLEDGE AND PREPARATION

Most people lack important retirement planning knowledge, according to the 2014 Retirement Income Literacy Survey conducted by the American College of Financial Planning. A *meager 20 percent* of respondents demonstrated basic knowledge skills in key retirement areas such as Social Security benefits, annuities, retirement investments, longevity, long-term-care planning and Walmart greeter skills (just kidding). Roughly 43 percent of Americans graded their financial knowledge at a C or below, according to the National Foundation for Credit Counseling. This is a matter of concern since most people rate themselves higher than they really are.

It turns out that lack of retirement knowledge is only part of a bigger problem. Of those questioned in the American College survey, a whopping 97 percent thought of themselves as "very knowledgeable" or "somewhat knowledgeable" about saving for a comfortable retirement. Yet only 27 percent of the self-proclaimed "very" or "somewhat knowledgeable" groups reported having a written retirement plan in place. Over half of these respondents said they had a relationship with a financial adviser. This last response implies that engaging a financial adviser may not always ensure that you will be encouraged to complete a written financial plan versus just having your retirement investment account managed by the adviser. Even more surprising, 52 percent of those surveyed said they were only moderately concerned about running out of money in retirement, yet 33 percent hadn't ever tried to establish how much money (a financial planning activity) they needed to accumulate for a secure retirement. It seems Blind Faith was not just the name of a rock group in the '60s!

A false sense of confidence can lead to costly, sometimes irreversible, mistakes. For example, a large majority of those surveyed in the American College survey were not aware of an important Social Security strategy. Specifically, waiting until age seventy to claim Social Security benefits provides a bonus of eight percent annually in annual income benefits plus cost-of-living increases. This increased amount affects not only the primary income benefit of the recipient for his or her lifetime but also spousal and surviving spouse benefits. Yet 60 percent of the respondents who failed to recognize the benefits of delaying Social Security payments said they have spent a lot of time thinking about when to claim Social Security benefits. It's important to know the facts before you decide on important issues like when to claim your Social

Security benefits. The folks at Social Security typically don't give you a do-over past the first year after selecting your benefit options unless you are willing and capable of paying all the money you received back to Social Security first.

Studies continue to reveal workers perform poorly as their own financial planners when managing their 401(k) accounts themselves, as evidenced by low or no contribution rates and often choosing inappropriate investment funds. This shortcoming can be traced to lack of basic financial planning education. In the past, when I conducted a short retirement-planning education workshop for a company's employees, 401(k) participation rates always went up after the program. It isn't that participants found more money to invest or that I threatened the noncontributors. Instead, they learned about the very real long-term benefits and absolute necessity of participating in a retirement savings plan. In essence, an increase in basic education helped them tune into everyone's favorite station—WIIFM—what's in it for me?

Even though recent regulation changes allow for new hires to be automatically enrolled by employers in their company 401(k) program when eligible, many new participants lack important financial knowledge and are unclear about appropriate contribution amounts and suitable investment choices. Also, some retirement plans allow for an automatic enrollment into a default investment fund for those new hires who don't elect their own investment choice from the menu of plan investment options. However, too many participants still don't fully understand what they actually own and why they own it.

For those who choose to select their own investments through an employer plan, many fail to maintain sufficient exposure to equities (stocks) in the early years of their employment; that means there's an increase in the risk of inflation dramatically affecting the purchasing power of these savings later on. Owning equities also provides an opportunity to accumulate additional money through long-term capital appreciation that the saver may not otherwise be able to put away on a limited budget. Some mistakenly choose overexposure to stocks in the last few years before retirement distributions begin, hoping to make up for lost time. The result of arriving at the equity investment party late is an increase in financial-market risk.

A basic question I don't often hear asked of a 401(k) participant is this: Why are you investing in this plan? Answers will vary—tax deductibility, tax deferral, employer match, retirement. These responses are all good reasons to participate. However, the last reason—retirement—should always be the primary reason. Why? For most people, investing in a 401(k) provides a significantly important future income replacement alternative for the dying, disappearing pension plan of past generations.

For those whose retirement goals are far off in the future, and if retirement income is the primary reason to participate in a 401(k), why are so many participants choosing the short-term investment option called "cash or stable value fund" rather than a longer-term, equity-based investment choice? The answer usually is this: "Well, because I don't want to lose any money." Fear of losing money is always a good reason to be cautious. But as a result, given a choice between predictability now versus later, the financially unaware will most always choose predictability now (a bird-in-the-hand syndrome) not realizing that, as a consequence, they are making their long-term goal of retirement-income predictability harder to achieve. The paradox is that the same investor who is risk averse and chooses short-term principal predictability (the cash or bond option) is actually putting purchasing power in later years at risk. Financially educated investors more often choose an investment strategy matched to their goal rather than their emotions. Those in the know accept short-term financial-market fluctuation as the emotional *cost* for greater long-term income certainty and the emotional benefit of peace-of-mind when they really need it.

Due to the complexities of choices when establishing and maintaining a 401(k) plan, employee participants with little or no investing experience and/or financial education would benefit greatly by seeking professional guidance from an experienced financial adviser.

Retirement-ready literacy is not just a matter of having or lacking knowledge of retirement account management of savings vehicles such as 401(k)s and IRAs. It's also a matter of depth or shortage of real-world practical knowledge in other important areas such as the huge benefits from annual tax planning, budgeting, and health-care insurance considerations. All of these components are critical to effectively planning for retirement years. Additionally, there are new developments in modern retirement planning, such as reverse-mortgage strategies and long-term-care hybrid insurance options that add to an already challenging learning curve. Remember early in this book, when you read that "retirement is no longer a predetermined destination"? If not already convinced of that statement, you may be beginning to understand why it's true. You can't go to and remain at retirement recess until your preparation homework is finished. Sooner is better than later!

EXTRA CREDIT

WWW.RETIREMENTRECESS.COM/RETIRE-READY-RESOURCE-CENTER

READ ROTH 401(K) VS. TRADITIONAL 401(K)

PROCRASTINATION

Another factor hampering retirement readiness is procrastination, or "I'll do my homework later." Remember how this worked out when you were in school? "Later" arrives sooner than anticipated and with it that awful, sinking feeling that accompanies lack of preparation before an important deadline—like the retirement-recess bell.

One possible reason for procrastinating on important actions like creating, funding, and protecting a retirement-recess financial plan is being overly confident about the future. It's human nature to hope that the future will be rosier than it might otherwise be without some intervention on your part to make it so. It's good to have a positive and hopeful attitude about the future. I'm a glass-half-full person myself. But don't let hope alone be the main driver of your future financial destiny. Hope can quickly become a distraction and an excuse to procrastinate and not take action, especially when hope is rooted in a false belief. I know a man who put off important actions to help secure a better financial future for himself and his family because of his false hope of winning the lotto. Every week he bought a ticket and fantasized about what he would do with the millions of dollars he would win. He dreamed about how he would be able to use part of the winnings to secure his financial independence and donate to charitable causes he cared about. Meanwhile, important time was slipping by, time he could have constructively used to prepare for his financial future rather than just hoping in vain for a better tomorrow. I explained it to him this way: Every week you are hoping to instantly obtain financial independence with no more effort than the time it takes to buy a lotto ticket with a one-dollar investment—an investment that has odds of one in a bazillion of paying off for you. In the meantime, each week you procrastinate in completing your financial homework, you are increasing the odds that you will become the opposite of what the lotto promises—that is, you are increasing the risk of becoming financially dependent on others for support. Go ahead and buy the ticket. Who knows? Maybe you will win the jackpot. But hedge your bets so that if you don't win—and the odds are astronomically great that you won't—you'll still have the backup of having done the right thing by completing the tasks that don't require luck to achieve.

Another cause of procrastination is the false belief that there will always be time to complete the goal in the future. Waiting even a year to begin a program of paying yourself first via a retirement account will increase the cost significantly.

To illustrate the cost of procrastination, meet Les the Procrastinator. Les plans to begin retirement recess in thirty years, when he is in his early sixties. He calculates he will need $1 million in retirement savings to supplement other retirement-income sources to fund his "later on" retirement-lifestyle goals. Like others his age, Les currently has not begun to save for this goal. He calculates if he uses his company 401(k) plan and chooses a growth investment allocation (80 percent stocks/20 percent bonds), he will be successful in reaching his goal provided he "pays himself first" a sufficient amount each month. Les knows that using a growth investment allocation will involve enduring the ups and downs of the variable stock market and will require some discipline to stay invested during periodic financial market declines. However, Les also knows that choosing a more predictable investment plan in the short-term (cash and bonds) will result in an increase in inflation risk later on. Les has wisely chosen retirement-income certainty (inflation protected) for the future rather than principal certainty (cash/bonds) in the short-term. To choose otherwise would require a much greater contribution amount on Les's behalf to keep pace with inflationary increases. Les does some research and decides it is reasonable to assume his investment choice will earn an average return of around 8 percent annually over the next thirty years. Always remember that assumed investment returns are just that, "assumed," and they are never guaranteed. Rather, they are used as an approximate investment-value outcome for planning purposes. As you know, actual investment returns will vary. If his assumption about return is accurate, Les will need to invest $671 each month to make his retirement-dream goal a reality. This annual contribution amount is approximately 10 percent of his current salary. Notice that the annual contribution amount, $8,052, multiplied by thirty years (the investment period) equals $241,560. The power of long-term compounding (assumed at 8 percent annually) will make up the difference between Les's pay-self-first contribution and his ultimate goal amount—$1 million. Einstein said, "Compound interest is the eighth wonder of the world. He who understands it, earns it . . . he who doesn't . . . pays it." If Les had chosen a more conservative investment choice that was more stable in the short-term, but only grew by half of his assumed investment return—4 percent—and he contributed the same $671 from his paychecks over the same thirty-year period, his account would be worth about $465,707—well short of his $1 million retirement goal. To make up the cost for a more conservative investment choice, Les would need to increase his monthly contribution amount from $671 to $1,441, well beyond his present monthly budget. It is important to review actual investment performance each year so adjustments can be made to contribution amounts and investment portfolios when needed. If Les's employer matched all or part of his contributions, his out-of-pocket requirement would be lower to meet his $1 million goal. Also, those figures don't include any future salary raises. If Les continues to contribute a percentage of salary rather than a fixed dollar amount, the raises will cause greater net contributions to his retirement-plan account than he is currently counting on. Finally,

Les will also receive income tax deductions each year for his qualified contributions. He estimates his combined marginal federal and state tax bracket to be 25 percent. At this rate, each $671 investment into his plan will save him $168 in taxes. These allowable deductions will lower his income-tax liability, producing more take-home cash to spend on other living expenses. This investment strategy represents a workable plan for someone who is serious about capturing a percentage of working income each year to fund future financial-independence goals. Sounds like a plan.

Let's check in with Les ten years later. He has been busy with career and personal life, and while enjoying the benefits of a rising income, he failed to pay himself first from each paycheck as he had planned ten years earlier. His belief: I have lots of time (twenty years remaining) to begin saving for my retirement. Les has become a victim of procrastination cost—believing he could still accomplish his goal over less time, Les learns a shocking truth. Even though he still has twenty years before he plans to retire and utilize these funds, if he still wants $1 million upon retirement, the new contribution amount has increased by over 250 percent to $1,698 monthly! His salary has not risen in equal measure, so the percentage of contribution compared to his current income is now much higher, making it more difficult, if not impossible, to budget the higher amount toward his retirement account. Les has also missed out on any employer-match contributions to his plan and on income-tax savings on qualified contribution amounts he would have enjoyed along the way. Les is wondering how failing to employ the eighth wonder of the world over the past ten years, which is only one-third of his thirty-year contribution period, could cost him so much that to make up for it he has to pay in over 250 percent in increased monthly contributions. His question can be answered in three words: *compounding and time*. Einstein was right—earn it or pay it. The loss of compounding money over time, especially over long periods, is huge. If Les can't come up with the additional discretionary income to afford the increased contribution amount, he will need to do the following:

1. Consider cutting back on nonessential expenses, which may degrade his lifestyle, to afford the new contribution amount, thus sacrificing short-term fun for long-term necessities. Boo!
2. Choose a more aggressive investment allocation, which may increase the risk of financial market fluctuation and asset allocation risk. Yikes!
3. Delay his retirement launch date, resulting in increased employment risk. Darn!

You will learn more about these choices and the previously mentioned risks that I call retirement income security killers (RISK) in a future chapter.

Moral of the story: Act now rather than later, especially on the things that need to be completed (like your financial homework) to achieve your most important lifetime goal—retirement recess. Most reformed procrastinators report that setting goals and breaking them down into small manageable action pieces is what gets them unstuck and moving forward. When progress is measurable, even in small amounts, you will begin to feel empowered rather than powerless.

TAKE NOTE

THE LONGER YOU WAIT TO BEGIN SAVING FOR A FUTURE GOAL, THE MORE MONEY IT WILL TAKE TO REACH THE SAME GOAL. RETIREMENT-PLANNING PROCRASTINATION LEADS TO POSTPONED GOAL ACHIEVEMENT. THE FURTHER OUT YOU PUSH YOUR RETIREMENT DATE, THE GREATER THE RISK OF RELYING ON OTHERS FOR FINANCIAL SUPPORT.

EXTRA CREDIT

WANT TO GIVE A MINOR CHILD/GRANDCHILD A HUGE TURBO BOOST ON HIS OR HER RETIREMENT SAVINGS? OPEN A RETIREMENT ACCOUNT AND CONTRIBUTE TO IT UNTIL THE RECIPIENT'S CAREER BEGINS. READ HOW IT WORKS AT WWW.RETIREMENTRECESS.COM/RETIRE-READY-RESOURCE-CENTER.

BAD LUCK

Another factor that can negatively affect retirement readiness is often referred to as "bad luck." Life happens. Circumstances and events that feel like bad luck will find all of us from time to time. Every experience, good or bad, has a life lesson to teach us. Often what we initially believe to be bad luck turns out to be something good in disguise, a path to something better down the road—maybe even good fortune. As we survive bad luck experiences, they usually make us stronger and hopefully wiser. Even the retirement-ready group has experienced a detour or two as they traveled the road to their financial independence destiny.

But is it really bad luck or simply bad preparation caused by lack of knowledge and procrastination that got the ball rolling toward a less-than-optimal result? When we examine unfortunate circumstances in finances more closely, we discover that many could have been less "unlucky" if a greater level of preplanning had been initiated beforehand. In other words, anticipate the event before it occurs and act to avoid, reduce, or eliminate the risk before it manifests in a full-blown bad luck consequence. I call this strategy "preemptive crisis management," or PCM.

For example, my wife, Carol, and I choose to live in a high-risk wildfire area in Colorado, not because we love forest fires but because we love the natural beauty and wildlife that surrounds our home. For those of us living in such areas, the time to begin a wildfire mitigation program is not when the flames are ten feet from the front door. PCM fire-risk mitigation is a year-round activity for us. Of course, mitigating fire risk doesn't guarantee that a wildfire won't burn down our home, but it can reduce the potential damage if a fire happens. Fire-mitigation efforts also allow us to feel like we have some control in what otherwise might be a powerless situation.

If our fire-mitigation efforts fail, and a wildfire destroys our home, we have transferred the risk of financial loss of the home structure and personal property to an insurance company that has contractually promised to pay for the rebuilding of the house and replace our stuff should a loss occur. This transfer of risk is paid for by our making an annual premium payment to an insurance company willing to assume the risk. Preemptive crisis management (PCM) for this bad luck possibility protects us financially as best it can if that event ever happens. We also have an expedited evacuation plan for the assets that money can't replace—like the humans and animals who occupy the home. The house can be rebuilt—not so much the people and animals who live within it.

From a financial planning point of view, PCM for potential financial risk can soften the blows when or if they do occur. To do so requires doing some homework to identify potential threats to your financial well-being and taking the appropriate steps to mitigate those threats when possible. You will learn about seventeen retirement income security killers (RISKs) and how to effectively mitigate them as you read on.

What seems like a bad luck experience is often the result of poor planning. Case in point: We often read about or know people who share personal "bad luck" stories about delaying their planned retirement-recess dates due to the negative financial consequences of the 2008–2010 Great Recession. The economic and near financial collapse that resulted from the events from that period was extreme and affected nearly everyone in some way. My question is this: Why did so many near-retirement folks have the portion of their retirement savings they relied upon to provide income for the first several years of their retirement invested in ways that were unprotected from the possibility of such events? Answers vary. The two most common responses I hear are these: I didn't know my investments could lose that much money so quickly, and I thought I could move my investments to a safer place before a crisis like this occurred. The first response is the result of the false belief that investments are somehow infallible against the forces (positive and negative) that affect them. The second response is rooted in the false belief, that the exact date of periodic financial market declines can be predicted with accuracy, thus giving you time to exit the market before the damage occurs. Although the mainstream media, journalists, and some financial advisers defend these beliefs with vigor, sooner or later investors and financial advisers alike must accept the *big truth* about the true nature of stock market investing if they are to reduce "bad luck" experiences from their financial lives. The big truth is this: Investing a portion of your serious retirement money in a well-diversified portfolio containing common stocks is a proven strategy to combat inflationary increases that rob future retirement income, especially over what could be a thirty-to forty year retirement period. However, no one can predict the time, direction, or magnitude of survivable financial market swings that occur along the way. Retirement investing requires you to accept uncertainty in the short-term (volatility) as the emotional cost for enjoying retirement-income certainty (due to capital growth and inflation protection) later on. To believe you can "time" the financial markets and avoid periodic market fluctuations while enjoying unabated long-term capital growth is to believe the big lie: I can, or someone I know can, predict the unpredictable.

Let's also give honorable mention to other PCM "musts" for successful investing: asset diversification; time; professional management—as in the hiring of someone other than your Aunt Gilda to save you from yourself when you forget the big truth; and a proven income-distribution strategy (created by you and/or your financial adviser) to weather the periodic financial market declines while simultaneously taking retirement-income distributions.

History is an excellent teacher and constant reminder, and although there is no absolute assurance it will repeat itself, it seems to do just that more than not. History shows us that while the stock market provides excellent long-term capital appreciation and long-term protection from increases in the future cost of living so necessary to fund a thirty-year retirement, it also experiences a significant decline in value every so often. From 1980 through 2016, the stock market as measured by the S&P 500 stock index has seen an average intra-year decline of 14% each year. Periodically, even greater intra-year declines can also occur. Although unnerving, these setbacks are normal occurrences. The duration of these declines varies from a few weeks to several years, and the time periods between fits of financial market negative volatility varies as well. For the broader diversified stock market (S&P 500), periodic financial-market declines have always recovered from their losses, as evidenced by an average 12.94 percent per year gain from 1980 through 2016. Note that "average" returns are derived from actual annual investment returns that are higher and lower, sometimes significantly so, than the average they create and never come with a repeat-performance promise. Also know that different investment periods can produce different results.

Normal periodic financial-market declines, by themselves, are not bad-luck experiences any more than a financial market gain is a good-luck experience. Both occur as the normal up and down trends of the financial markets. What you decide to do as a result will determine your consequences more than superstitiously believing that luck, good or bad, played a part. Over long periods of time, financial markets as a whole rise more than they fall. The potential gains created by these differences is the profit that makes possible the ability to one day convert capital appreciation into inflation-protected retirement-income dollars. Implementing a PCM investment income distribution strategy to protect retirement account principal during periodic financial- market declines is imperative to your financial health during retirement.

Learning and practicing preemptive crisis management (PCM) strategies for retirement investment accounts and other components of comprehensive retirement planning covered in this book may not change your luck, but they will help to ensure that your ultimate success in becoming retirement-recess ready isn't based on luck alone.

TAKE NOTE

THE BIG TRUTH: ALTHOUGH INVESTING A PORTION OF YOUR SERIOUS RETIREMENT MONEY IN COMMON STOCKS IS A PROVEN STRATEGY TO COMBAT INFLATIONARY INCREASES THAT ROB FUTURE RETIREMENT INCOME, NO ONE CAN PREDICT THE TIME, DIRECTION, OR MAGNITUDE OF FINANCIAL-MARKET VALUE SWINGS IN THE SHORT-TERM EXPERIENCED BY THIS ASSET CLASS WITH COMPLETE ACCURACY. LONG-TERM SUCCESS IN RETIREMENT INVESTING REQUIRES THAT YOU ACCEPT ACCOUNT-VALUE UNCERTAINTY IN THE SHORT-TERM (VOLATILITY) AS PAYMENT FOR RETIREMENT-INCOME CERTAINTY (INFLATION PROTECTION) LATER ON WHEN YOU MOST NEED IT.

Why bother with all this fuss? Why not just deposit 100 percent of your retirement savings in a good ol' principal-safe account such as a money market or savings account when you retire? In other words, put all your retirement savings in the storm cellar regardless of the financial weather outside. I'll answer in five words: No long-term inflation protection. Unless you have ample funds already saved for future inflationary increases over the next thirty years, or if you don't intend to live very long (be careful with this assumption), you are making a costly exchange—trading increased account-value certainty in the short-term for decreased income-purchasing-power certainty in the long-term. Believe the words of retirees who have gone before you when they report that the continued rise in their cost of living, while living on mostly fixed income in later years, is something they wished they had better planned for prior to ringing their retirement-recess bell.

TAKE NOTE

IF YOU WANT TO CHANGE YOUR LUCK, PLAN AHEAD FOR THE EVENTS AND CIRCUMSTANCES THAT ARE IDENTIFIABLE AS POTENTIAL RISKS BEFORE, NOT AFTER, THEY OCCUR. IN OTHER WORDS, PRACTICE PREEMPTIVE CRISIS MANAGEMENT.

FEAR

Another reason so many people are unprepared financially and emotionally to fully enjoy their retirement lifetimes is due to a force they are afraid to admit—fear. Ask a room full of second-graders who want to go to recess, and every hand will enthusiastically shoot up into the air, with half the class running for the door. Ask a room full of fifty-something workers who wants to retire, and the response is mixed. Some enthusiastically raise their hands but have no idea what their projected retirement lifestyle really looks like. Others respond to this question as if they were asked how they feel about a root canal. The lack of financial preparation and fear of the unknown has many retirement hopefuls pondering their financial futures with much trepidation.

It's human nature to fear the unknown. For most people, the whole idea of retirement is an entirely new concept that they have never tackled before. A huge fear associated with retirement, second only to running out of money, is this: Will I still find meaning, purpose, and independence in my life after I retire from my all-too-familiar, work-for-a-living-lifestyle routines? In short, "Will I still be relevant?"

Fear of the unknown, whether conscious or not, has the power to prevent us from taking the necessary steps to create, fund, and protect the fulfilling lifestyle that we ultimately seek. An antidote to financial fear involves unmasking both financial planning uncertainties *and* lifestyle-planning unknowns associated with retirement. In doing so, many discover new possibilities for relevance in retirement, including empowerment where they once feared powerlessness, connectivity where they once feared isolation, and individuality where they once feared conformity.

TAKING A FEAR INVENTORY

> I've lived through some terrible things in my life,
> some of which actually happened.
> - Mark Twain

Psychological research studies reveal that 85 percent of what people worry about never actually happens. Of the 15 percent of worrisome events that do occur, most result in handling the difficulty better than expected, or the difficulty itself provides a basis for a lesson worth learning. This being said, remember that fear most often occurs as an irrational emotion. Attempting to logically explain away the illogical emotion of fear is like whistling in the dark, pretending you have courage when you really don't. The fear is still present, but at least you're sounding like it's not! It's also important to note that being a little worried about important things like the solvency of your retirement years and who you will *be* once you retire can prove to be a good motivator to take positive steps forward. Yet if you allow the fear of your future retirement finances and unknown retirement lifestyle to freeze you up from taking essential steps, fear is controlling your future outcomes in a negative way. There is a big difference between being motivated by fear and frozen by fear.

Completing a periodic financial-fear-inventory exercise can prove very useful in discovering the root cause(s) of your fear and, more importantly, it can help you realize how we all are empowered to overcome our fears once we have the courage to face them.

Fear, financial or otherwise, most often is rooted in false beliefs. When we examine why we tend to believe something to be true or not, many times we find that we are still clinging to beliefs that are way past their expiration dates. In other words, they may have been applicable in the past, but not anymore. A perfect example is found by examining beliefs about what our retirement lifestyle will actually look like. Old retirement-lifestyle beliefs centered around being old, worn out, or obsolete. Who wants to work and save toward this end? Much of what you are reading in this book is about planning and living an empowered, dynamic retirement lifestyle that is anything but obsolete. Recess for grown-ups equates to being active, creative, and engaging, not boring, restrictive, and dull.

The word "fear" can be treated as an acronym for false evidence appearing real. From my own personal experience, when our fears are faced, they, not we, most often run for the exits.

Homework:

Complete the financial-fear inventory exercise.

You will find this homework assignment in the *Retirement Recess Homework/Exercise Workbook,* available at www.retirementrecess. com. You can also copy each of the following questions on a blank sheet of paper. Leave lots of space between each question for your answers.

What is my greatest financial fear?

When did I first become aware of this fear?

How is this fear affecting me today?

What is the lie I am telling myself as a result of this fear?

How do I perpetuate this lie in my daily life?

What can I do instead?

Find a quiet time where you won't be interrupted for fifteen to twenty minutes. Take a few deep breaths and clear your mind. Ask yourself each fear question out loud. Write down your response to each question. Do not judge your answers as "good" or "bad" or "right" or "wrong." Also, don't try to overthink your responses.

Example-Fear-Inventory Assignment:

What is my greatest financial fear? *Financial dependence on others during my retirement years.*

When did I first become aware of this fear? *Unknown. Witnessed a relative who spent entire retirement feeling obsolete. Also, read about people who are depleting their savings in retirement and becoming dependent on others.*

How is this fear affecting me today? *Keeps me from taking appropriate action(s). Excess worry about the future. Added stress. Afraid to spend money now. I don't feel I can afford to make a mistake, so I do nothing.*

What's the lie I am telling myself as a result of this fear? *That I can never obtain financial independence.*

How do I perpetuate this lie in my daily life? *Procrastination. Avoidance. Excuses.*

What can I do instead? *Read the remainder of this book. Seek a financial professional who will hold me accountable for my actions and commitments. Make a commitment to move forward even when I feel uncomfortable. Believe it is possible to improve my financial independence capabilities. Become a student of my financial future. Complete a retirement-life-planning exercise and all homework assignments recommended in this book.*

Complete a separate fear inventory sheet for as many financial fears as you presently have. It might be helpful to take a fear inventory periodically or whenever you begin to feel yourself freezing up and not taking action on a financial matter.

Now that you have more information about the forces that hinder retirement success—lack of knowledge, procrastination, "bad luck," and fear—make a commitment to yourself and your family right now to move beyond these roadblocks. For those who don't, the next chapter is for you.

Chapter Four

The Great American Default Retirement Plan: "I'll Just Keep Working"

For those who fail to finish their retirement-planning homework on time, there is a default retirement plan called "I'll just keep working." Although the trend for continued employment in later years is rising, doing so without a standby retirement-income plan (one you can immediately switch on when employment income switches off) can be hazardous to your financial future.

Recent information provided by the Center for Retirement Research at Boston College confirms two important trends: The primary reason people choose to work past traditional retirement ages is lack of financial preparation. Changes in health (the worker's or a family member's) are the number one reason why workers retire earlier than planned.

Age at Which Worker Intend to Retire

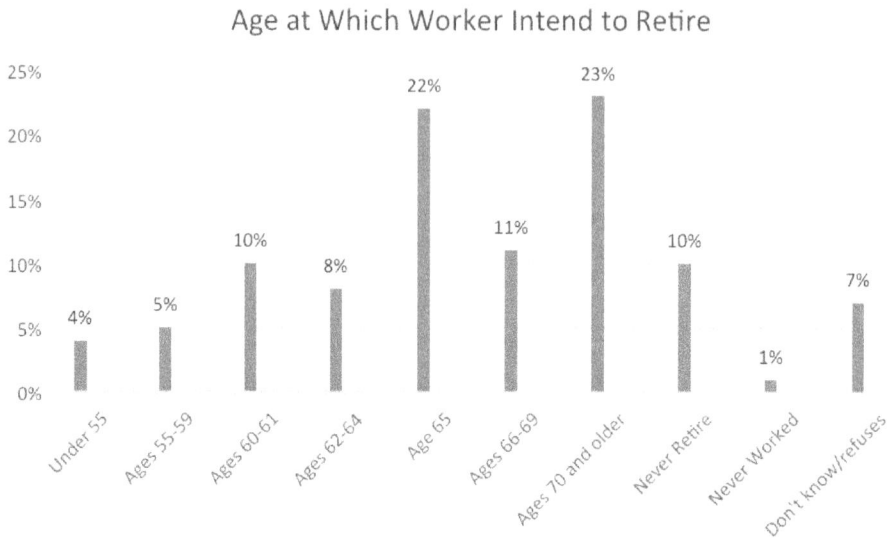

Chart Source: Information provided by Employee Benefit Research Institute, 2015

A 2015 survey conducted by the Employee Benefit Research Institute (EBRI) asked workers when they intended to retire. Only 27 percent of those surveyed said they were planning to retire before age sixty-five. A whopping 44 percent said they intended to retire at an age older than sixty-five, including 10 percent who said they would never retire, which evidently meant that they intended to die on the job, or so they hoped.

As we discussed earlier, it's important to remember that just because someone "intends" to retire by a certain age, that doesn't necessarily mean that person will be able to actually fulfill that intention.

Many who must continue to work because they lack the financial means to support themselves in their later years are doing so because they have to, not because they want to. The difference between *having* to work and *wanting* to work is huge from a financial security and emotional standpoint. Wanting to work means you enjoy the emotional and financial rewards of continued employment, preferably mixed with plenty of play periods (retirement recess). Having to work equates to this: Because of the choices I've made or not made in the past, I simply have no other choice but to continue working to provide for my immediate and future financial support. This result produces no real financial security past the next paycheck. The fate of the next payday is dependent on your physical and mental capacity to continue to do the tasks your job requires. Another factor to consider when continuing to work into later years is the likelihood that your employer and coworkers may be considerably younger than you. One later-life worker confided she was not emotionally prepared to be reporting to a supervisor who was younger than her son!

In addition to financial reasons for continued employment, the following is a list of current trends that contribute to staying on the job longer:

- **Improved Health and Longevity:** The correlation between improving health at later stages of life and continued employment is strong.
- **Less Physically Demanding Jobs:** With the shift away from manufacturing, jobs now involve more knowledge-based activities that put less strain on older bodies. Many people make the transition from labor-intense to less-stressful employment positions to increase their ability to continue to work longer.
- **Decline of Retiree Health Insurance:** Combine the decline of employer-provided retirement health insurance with the rapid rise in private health-care costs, and workers have a strong incentive to keep working and maintaining their employer's health coverage until they qualify for Medicare at age sixty-five.
- **Identity:** Who will I be when I'm no longer doing what I do for a living? Career years provide an identity and purpose in life.

Those who have not completed retirement-life-planning homework continue to find their primary identity in their work life.

- **Social:** What fun is retirement recess when everyone else is still in the classroom working? Community aspects of the work environment are highly important. When someone retires and leaves the social network at work behind, that person is no longer a part of the social circle of active employees. Some find this prospect dreadful while others find it emancipating.

Your efforts to mitigate the risk associated with working at older ages is paramount to lowering the odds of an early spend down of assets if you should have to leave employment before you are ready.

PLAN TO WORK LONGER IF YOU WISH BUT BE FINANCIALLY PREPARED TO RETIRE SOONER IF AND WHEN CIRCUMSTANCES BEYOND YOUR CONTROL PREVAIL.

Chapter Five

Planning for Retirement Recess

Depending on your level of preparation, your retirement story will either be written by you or by fate—it's your choice. Either way, retirements are planned for the future, not the past. Gone for most folks are the relics of retirement past—the symbolic gold watch and living worry-free on retirement income provided by a solvent Social Security and company pension machine that spits out retirement-income checks for as long as you live.

Improvements in health care, public sanitation, lifestyle, and technology are rapidly increasing the years of life expectancy worldwide; concurrently, traditional retirement-income sources to fund these additional years are not keeping pace with the demands that longevity is creating. The longevity income gap (the gap between how long you live and how long your money lasts) created by these two diverging trends is not asking for but demanding that we consider new ways of thinking and planning to replace the outdated retirement planning strategies of past generations. Bob Dylan was right: "The times they are a-changin'." So must we.

A PURPOSE-FULL LIFE

What will be your new purpose during your retirement-recess years? Will you choose to spend extended time with those you love? Maybe you will donate your time, skills, and money to social or environmental causes you've always cared about but didn't have the time to pursue during your working years. Perhaps you may decide to reinvent yourself completely or continue building on your current identity as a work in progress. Will you be one of those who enjoy a permanent thirty-year play vacation? Or will you choose a mix of recess play periods and continued employment stints—either working for someone else or for a new start-up employer named *You Inc.*?

These are a few of the important retirement lifestyle questions that need your careful thought and consideration long before the retirement-recess bell rings. Whatever you decide, one thing is for sure: *you can't go to recess until your homework is finished.*

WHAT HOMEWORK?

The world's most lavish playgrounds for grown-ups are eagerly awaiting your arrival. But your retirement-recess ambitions won't happen without first getting your financial and emotional retirement-planning homework finished.

Retirement-planning homework consists of more than just managing your IRA. It involves creating your retirement-lifestyle vision (your new purpose) and taking the appropriate steps to not just fully fund your vision with retirement savings but also to protect it from risks that threaten an early spend down of your financial resources. As you know, an early asset spend down results in an end to recess time and a loss of financial independence. If you are an emoji person, insert a sad face here.

You may be thinking, "My parents (or someone else you know who is retired) didn't complete any homework before their retirement date, and they made out just fine." Maybe so, but remember, you are not planning or living their retirement. Retirement readiness is no longer an automatic rite of passage from a working career to a guaranteed life of leisure. Here is your review list of the changing dynamics that are altering the way we must plan for today's retirement:

- Longer life expectancy (bonus or bust years)
- Reduced or no pension income benefit availability
- Questionable Social Security sustainability
- Dramatically rising health-care costs
- Increasing demand by retirees for a more active lifestyle
- Increased likelihood of providing financial support for aging parents and/or adult children who failed to launch into their own independent lifestyle

TAKE NOTE

THE QUALITY OF YOUR RETIREMENT-RECESS PERIOD IS DIRECTLY PROPORTIONAL TO THE AMOUNT OF FINANCIAL AND EMOTIONAL PREPARATION YOU COMPLETE BEFORE THE RETIREMENT-RECESS BELL RINGS.

DO YOU NEED A WRITTEN, COMPREHENSIVE RETIREMENT FINANCIAL PLAN?

If you don't already have a written financial plan, a good question is—why not? Thanks to modern technology, the ability to design and create a professionally written plan that addresses all your goals and concerns has never been easier or more affordable to obtain.

Unfortunately, there is no standard model that determines how comprehensive a financial plan should be for a particular person's situation. Financial advisers' opinions vary greatly regarding the depth and scope of what a financial plan should or should not include. Unlike an income tax return that uses the same forms for different tax filers, one person could go to three different financial planners and leave with three different versions of a financial plan. Some financial plans focus on managing investments while other plans might focus on the need to own life insurance. Both of these components—asset management and life insurance assessment—are important pieces of a comprehensive financial plan, but other areas of planning are equally important to your financial health. You will learn about all of them shortly.

There are usually three common responses to "do you need a professionally written, comprehensive financial plan?" 1.) No, I do it myself. 2.) Yes, but I don't know where to begin. 3.) I'm not sure; what's involved?

If you are a member of response group number one, welcome. You are probably reading this book as part of your ongoing research to further your retirement-readiness knowledge or to just check in and see if you are missing anything important thus far. For the price of this book and homework workbook and the time to read and complete each, I hope you find that your small investment has paid big dividends in knowledge that will help you obtain and remain at the highest level of retirement readiness. As a self-directed manager of your retirement affairs, you are a member of an elite group that truly has mastered what needs to be known to become and remain financially independent. And you have the focus to take necessary actions to succeed. You possess the knowledge, experience, discipline, and motivation to consistently remain updated and informed about important and ever-changing retirement-readiness trends. I recommend you bookmark and periodically reconnect to the website www.retirementrecess.com for updates and additional educational information, which will be posted when available. I also hope you pass along a copy of this book to someone you know who may not be as well-equipped as you so that person too may improve his or her own retirement prospects.

Those in response group number two know or feel they need help but don't know where to turn to obtain it or who they can trust to begin the important process of financial planning for their retirement. For this group, I've dedicated an entire chapter to help you locate, vet, interview, and hire a lifetime financial adviser (LFA). As you will learn, an LFA is a professional hired by you to assist in successfully navigating the increasingly complex maze of retirement-planning topics. Although I've defined and promoted the ideals of a lifetime financial adviser, remember my promise to you in the beginning? This book is not an infomercial about hiring me or someone I know personally as your LFA. However, I have included extensive financial adviser vetting (investigating) instructions to help guide you in the direction of a reputable professional. I encourage you to use my description of what an ideal lifetime financial planner looks, sounds, and acts like and to go through the Seven Cs Financial Adviser Evaluation to help you find your perfect match.

Finally, for those relating to response number three and wondering what's involved in financial planning, as I previously stated, there are many descriptions and practice standards for the financial planning process. Some are very comprehensive while others, quite honestly, only address a portion of what is considered the process of authentic retirement financial planning. As you read on, you will learn more about the necessary components of a real and comprehensive financial plan. The added homework assignments are there to assist you and your financial adviser (if applicable) as tools to work through the financial planning process to better prepare you to fully enjoy your retirement-recess adventure.

Chapter Six

Financial Planning: Science or Art?

Financial planning is both art and science. The science of financial planning includes gathering and analyzing information about assets, debts, insurance, estate documents, tax returns, future values for pensions (if applicable), Social Security, other income sources, and spending budgets. If you need them, blank sample worksheets are included in the *Retirement Recess Homework Workbook.* This is the business end of retirement planning. After compiling all your financial data, different strategies for saving and investing can be considered and tested as well as methods for converting and distributing assets for income while lowering tax costs when possible. With the aid of professional financial planning programs, participants can quickly analyze "what if" scenarios that simulate potential outcomes during different economic and spend down periods. There are certain questions that are best answered as a result of considering all the information about you and your unique goals beforehand. Those questions might include the following: How much do I need to save? How should I be invested?

What strategy is right for my income-distribution goals? Stress testing (simulating hypothetical risk factors) to determine whether a potential strategy will work prior to implementing it can prove invaluable.

Living in retirement affords few, if any, do-overs. Commercial pilots train in flight simulators for a similar reason—when situations arise that threaten the safety of the flight, there are few or no do-overs in actual flight. The science of financial planning by simulation before "going live" in the real retirement world helps determine the probable result of a proposed action or strategy before it is implemented as your planning policy.

Airline pilots also use checklists to verify that the configuration of the aircraft is correct before takeoff and landing. As routine as commercial flight has become, it's interesting that these checklists are still so important to flight safety. An experienced pilot will tell you that the routine aspect of flying is exactly why these checklists are so important. Overlook a step, and the entire safety of the flight could be at risk. A comprehensive financial plan should include a retirement-plan checklist as an important assessment tool to confirm that all pertinent planning steps are taken prior to and not after your retirement commencement date is cleared for takeoff.

TAKE NOTE

KNOWING HOW MUCH MONEY YOU NEED TO FULLY FUND YOUR RETIREMENT LIFESTYLE IS THE SINGLE MOST IMPORTANT FACTOR IN SHAPING YOUR FUTURE RETIREMENT DESTINY, YET IT'S THE LEAST-KNOWN PIECE OF INFORMATION AMONG THE PRERETIRED POPULATION.

The art of financial planning encourages us to look beyond the science of black-and-white (and occasionally red) columns of numbers and helps us dream about the feelings of financial freedom we have not felt in many years, if ever at all. It is the art of creating your retirement-lifestyle vision, not the science of financial planning, that stokes the fires of emotions and inspires the actions necessary so that one day we actually experience what we have envisioned in our imaginations for so long.

TAKE NOTE

THE SCIENCE OF RETIREMENT PLANNING CREATES THE FINANCIAL BORDERS OF YOUR RETIREMENT LIFESTYLE; THE ART OF RETIREMENT PLANNING FILLS IN THE SHAPE WITH VIBRANT, RICH COLORS AS YOU DESCRIBE IN DETAIL WHAT YOU WANT TO BE, DO, AND HAVE DURING YOUR RETIREMENT-RECESS TIME.

The process of imagining the details of a plan for living (the art) becomes more prevalent as you move through your working career and approach your retirement-recess age goal. If you are decades away from the retirement-recess bell, you will most likely be focusing more on the science rather than the art of retirement planning. At younger ages, your financial plan may consist solely of contributing as much of your wages as you can afford into a tax-deferred/tax-free retirement-plan investment account and living within your financial means (which includes managing debt). As your retirement-recess age draws nearer, you will become increasingly aware of glimpses of a lifestyle vision you aspire to experience, much like a painter envisioning and sketching a picture long before the shapes and colors appear on canvas.

TAKE NOTE

A GREAT RETIREMENT FINANCIAL PLAN SHOULDN'T BE DEFINED BY THE NUMBER OF PAGES IT CONTAINS. RATHER, IT SHOULD BE EVALUATED ON HOW EFFECTIVELY THE PLAN REDUCES THE RISKS OF AN EARLIER-THAN-PLANNED SPEND DOWN OF ASSETS OVER A RETIREMENT LIFETIME. IT IS BOTH THE SCIENCE AND ART OF FINANCIAL PLANNING THAT PROVIDES AN EFFECTIVE PROCESS TO ACCOMPLISH THIS GOAL.

Chapter Seven

Creating Your Future Life Plan

Of those who are saving for retirement, many have no idea what the life they are saving for might actually look like. More than saving for a "rainy day," they are saving for a thirty-year-long lifestyle that extends over 10,950 days of both sunshine and rain.

It is vital to describe as specifically as you can the lifestyle you are envisioning and at what age you would like the recess bell to ring. If you are already retired, consider what you want the next chapters of your retirement lifetime to look like. Once your retirement vision is out of your head and written down on paper (a matter of art), you are ready to create a financial plan to fund and protect it (a matter of science).

In some instances, the science of retirement planning is as far as many people and financial advisers get before they call the plan finished. Too many outdated lifestyle assumptions are made based on old retirement expectations (false beliefs) that simply do not apply to today's retirement realities. Remember, this is not someone else's retirement; it's yours.

To make retirement dreams real, we must begin to think beyond the science of financial data and awaken the lifestyle possibilities that slumber within. Although the financial calculations play a critical role and provide the "ways and means" of ensuring that money lasts as long as you do (and beyond if you have legacy wishes), equally important is the creative art of envisioning what your retirement lifestyle looks, tastes, smells, sounds, and feels like. After all, longevity trends say the odds are increasing every year that you are going to be spending a lot of time somewhere. Why not design a plan that fits your real desires rather than settling for someone else's worn-out vision, or worse, no vision at all?

One of my favorite retirement lifestyle visions was shared by a woman I know who simply said, "I want enough money saved by the time I retire to be able to travel to new and exotic destinations . . . and leave the return ticket dates open." Now that's a retirement recess! She built an entire retirement financial plan around this single state-ment. Of course, she had other goals and specific details that defined her retirement life, but the money she was investing throughout her working years wasn't earmarked to just increase her net worth in retire-ment; it was being invested to purchase her financial freedom. She's not retired; she's at recess!

WHEN YOU CHANGE THE PERCEPTION OF THE WAY YOU ASSUME THINGS WILL BE, AND OPEN YOUR MIND TO THE POSSIBILITIES, THE OPPORTUNITIES TO EXPERIENCE THEM DIFFERENTLY BEGIN TO APPEAR.

A LESSON IN RETIREMENT LIFESTYLE PERCEPTION: TRADING MOLARS FOR MUSKIES

Tom was a dentist, and Alice was a full-time homemaker until their retirement-recess bell rang several years ago. Today they live, play, and work as private resort owners on a small fly-in island on Lake of the Woods, Canada.

Growing up, Tom's perception of his destiny was he would graduate from high school, go to college, and then attend dental school just like his dad before him. It seemed his career path was decided before he was born. He woke up one morning after working for several years as a dentist and realized he hated what he did for a living. The love of his life—besides Alice—was fishing. In fact, he was so naturally good at it that a fishing tackle company consulted with Tom to create a line of fishing tackle with his name on it.

After many soul-searching conversations, Tom and Alice began to change their perceptions of what their future lifestyle could look like. Getting close to the age when most of their friends were beginning to think about traditional retirement lifestyles, Tom and Alice pursued a new way of living in retirement that included doing what they loved rather than what was expected.

One thing led to another, and before they knew it, the opportunity appeared to purchase a small resort where Tom visited during fishing respites from his dental practice. After much financial planning, consideration, and information gathering, they took the giant leap, sold the dental practice, bought the fishing resort, and opened for business. Tom manages the resort operations, including guided fishing trips on the lake, while Alice manages reservations, runs the kitchen for guest meals, and supervises the housekeeping staff. Tom and Alice are not retired; they are at recess!

RETIREMENT LIFESTYLE PERCEPTIONS—PAST AND PRESENT

> The greatest discovery of my generation is that human beings can alter their lives by altering their attitudes of mind.
> —William James

It's time we modernize our definitions and dated perceptions of what the lifestyle of retirement really is versus what it was. In the past, the idea of retirement signaled the beginning of the end. Today, it marks the beginning of a new and very active extended lifestyle. In the past, retirement meant being permanently resigned from a career. Today, an increasing number of people retire and then "rehire" themselves into new and dynamic careers and businesses, some for pay and some to simply pay their good fortune forward. In the past, retirement implied elderly and worn-out. Today, thanks to longer life expectancies and an improving quality of life, retirement signifies new and exciting chapters in the continuing story of you.

Homework:
Define what the word "retirement"
means to you.

Create your own synonyms for the word "retirement." Write down your answers. Examples include: retirement equals inspirement; overtime on my terms; the best second half of life; unsupervised playtime; recreating and re-creating. Email your "retirement" definitions to me at jim@retirementrecess.com, and I will share them with others who are also completing this assignment.

COMPLETING THE PICTURE

It's human nature to overlook important details when visualizing a future lifestyle you haven't experienced yet. We tend to collect visual pieces in our minds of what we imagine our future life will look like, but we don't always put all the pieces together and bring the big picture into clearer focus. Activities like playing golf or tennis describe a part of a retirement-lifestyle picture, but these activities are not the complete picture of your future-life vision.

Think of your retirement-lifestyle vision as a jigsaw puzzle. The first step in assembling the puzzle is to spread all the pieces face up on the table and then begin to connect them together, beginning with the borders, in such a way that each piece fits into another and creates a complete picture. Imagine trying to assemble a puzzle without knowing what the picture looks like ahead of time, or worse yet, if some of the pieces are missing.

Don't expect the advertising industry to help you define your retirement-lifestyle vision. It seems every week a new advertisement debuts with this message: Your retirement is_____. (Fill in the blank with an activity or event.) The active couple running on the beach (in slow motion) on a bright sunny morning is a wonderfully choreographed vision of an activity—it's a piece of the picture, but it's not the entire picture. The ad is selling a product or service related to a moment during retirement by connecting a product or service to a joyful event. That's not a problem unless you begin to believe a single event will define your lifestyle vision. Although running on the beach on a sunny morning every day of your retirement-recess period is a wonderful ideal, it is not a realistic expectation, especially over a span of several decades; that's a lot of running.

A well-thought-out lifestyle vision, accompanied by a written financial plan, is the ticket giving you entry to the life *you* create. As noted earlier, it's what I call *You Vision*.

When imagining your own retirement lifestyle, it may be helpful to think of people you know who are currently living a retirement life you admire. What do you like and dislike about their choices? Don't judge their decisions as good or bad; just observe what they consider important and decide if this is something you wish to replicate in your vision plan.

Homework:
Make some popcorn and watch a movie or two about lifestyles in retirement.

A couple of my favorites are these: *The Intern, Cocoon, On Golden Pond,* and *About Schmidt.* What do you like and dislike about other retirement lifestyles? Write down your thoughts and feelings.

Homework:
Ask yourself this: What am I retiring from and what am I retiring to?

Do you want to retire from something, like a job environment you dislike or even hate? Or do you want to retire to something new and different? Maybe it's a second chance at a new career. How about living in a different part of the country or world where the climate and lifestyle is perceived as more suitable for you? Climate is now second to affordability on the short list as a primary reason to relocate in retirement. Make a "retiring from and retiring to" list to help provide clues as to the lifestyle direction you imagine your retirement journey might take.

Homework:

Create or collect pictures from magazines and the internet that graphically illustrate what you want your retirement recess to look like.

Paste them on a presentation board for viewing or upload them to Pinterest. Make sure every area of your life is represented by this collage that describes where you will live, play, work, rest, grow, share, and just be.

Email your visual collage to jim@retirementrecess.com. I will post it on our web page called "Retirement—You Vision" so others can be inspired by your visuals and create their own.

CREATING YOUR UNIQUE LIFESTYLE VISION CALLED "YOU VISION"

Below is an illustration of the allocation of each area of an ideal retirement lifestyle. This is your life-facet allocation model. Similar to an investment asset allocation pie, it is made up of slices that collectively define a multidimensional, purposeful life.

The process of creating You Vision involves thinking about and defining what each life facet means to you. If you share your life with a partner/ spouse/significant other, I suggest both of you complete this exercise independently of each other and, when finished, share your completed life-facet allocation exercise together. You will be looking for common ground that you can share together, and you'll be identifying independent activities/interests that you might want to pursue separately.

You Vision—Life Facet Allocation

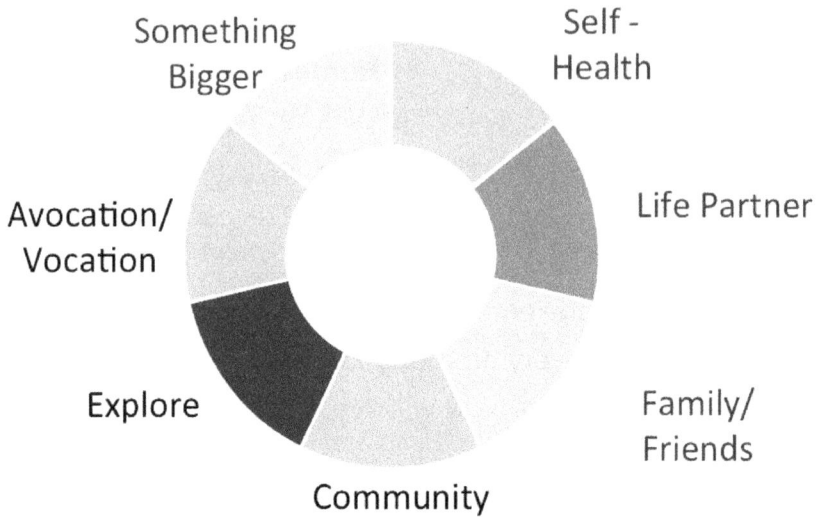

Something Bigger

Self - Health

Avocation/ Vocation

Life Partner

Explore

Family/ Friends

Community

BE, DO, AND HAVE

During career-building years, it is often believed that what we *have* (measured by material wealth/status) is the result of what we *do* (career), and once we *have* as a consequence of what we *do*, we will *be* (identity) somebody. Ask someone who they are, and often they respond by describing what they do for a living, not who they are as a person. For those who don't know yet, it's time to discover your true identity. Hint: It's not the title on your business card.

What Do You Want to Be?

To begin, let's reverse the order of *do–have–be* to *be–do–have*. First, consider what you want to *be* during your retirement lifetime. Think of what you want to *be* as an affirmation of your true identity. In other words, what you aspire to be. One way to accomplish this is to consider what you want to *be* remembered for. This is your legacy goal, and as you will see, it's very important to each life facet or slice of your retirement-lifestyle vision.

The top two regrets of those lying on their deathbed are these:

1. I wish I'd had the courage to live a life true to myself, not the life others expected of me.
2. I wish I hadn't worked so hard.

Beginning today, we all have the ability, through the power of choice, to live the remainder of our lives with no regrets. Whatever we decide to "be," whether it's someone who is true to self or perhaps someone remembered for certain unique traits, we are all empowered to effect change beginning with our own lives.

When considering how you want to *be* remembered, begin with the end of your life story. I call this the "tombstone test." Century-old cemetery headstones often described lifetime values by inscriptions of how lives were lived. Hundreds of years later, we read these insightful epitaphs etched in stone and admire the simple and pure values that live on long after the body is gone. I love the message on a headstone I saw while visiting Boston a few years ago: "Pardon my dust." It's a reminder to not take ourselves so seriously—because no one else does. I would have liked to have hung out with this guy during the colonial period in Boston.

What do you want inscribed on your tombstone? When the question is framed this way, it's interesting how the answers about what's really important to you emerge. I've never met anyone yet who wanted his or her legacy tombstone message to read "Retired" or "Wealthy." More likely, the responses to the tombstone question are value and character-based descriptions such as "Loving Husband/ Wife/Grandparent," "Caring Dad/Mom," "Giver," "Lifetime Friend," or "Unfailing keeper of the faith." I know one individual who simply stated, "I want to be remembered for really being 'present' for my family and friends. After a lifetime of being somewhere else, it's time to really be there with and for them." This is a great example of a values-based lifestyle vision statement.

What Do You Want to Do?

When people are asked this question relative to their retirement dreams, often their response is a description of an activity, like "play more golf" or "travel." It's important to know that although these activities may be part of your retirement-lifestyle goals, they are not the sum total of what your life represents. Activities such as sports, travel, education, and the like belong in the "explore" slice of your retirement-life plan. In addition to the explore slice of life, there are six additional life facets within a typical retirement-life plan. They are self/ health, life partner, family/friends, community, vocation/avocation, and something bigger.

Think of what you *do* as a commitment to support your *be* affirmations. The answer to the "what will I do" question within each life facet is connected to the "what will I be" answers. If you want to *be* a caring and loving grandparent in the family/friends component of your life, you will most likely find yourself defining several *do* actions that will help you *be* a caring and loving grandparent. Remember: Lasting impressions are those solidified by actions rather than by good intentions alone. To actualize, you must first visualize and verbalize.

If you are planning on a new and different career as a *be* response within your vocation/avocation facet, list the things you need to *do* to prepare for it—the education classes, experience, and people you should know. Is there someone you are aware of who is already doing what you want to do for work during retirement? Find out specifically what that person did, and use what you discover as a template for your own design.

What Do You Want to Have?

Finally, what do you want to *have* in retirement? It's common for people to respond to this question with an answer that defines an amount of money. Money is important. It may not buy you happiness, but it certainly buys you choices that can lead to greater happiness. The science of financial planning (financial calculations) will help in discovering how much money will be needed to keep your dreams afloat on the sea of your longevity. Notice I said "afloat" and not "adrift." Let's focus on what you want to have in life, in addition to enough money, to fulfill your lifestyle-retirement-recess goals. Think of *have* as the specific experience you seek for each area of your life. What you *have* is the result of what you decide to *be* and *do*.

Remember that the assets that money can't buy—such as good health, peace, joy, family, and faith—will be dearly missed after they are gone. Preserving your financial wealth is critically important to the success of your financial independence in retirement, but be careful to not overlook protecting the things that money can't buy, especially while you're still working, accumulating the capital to fund your retirement goals.

The responses to what you want to *be*, *do*, and *have* throughout your retirement years is as unique as your DNA. The only limits are your mental and physical health, your financial resources, and your willingness to play in all parts of your life regardless of your age. By the way, if you didn't know your actual age, how old would you say you are?

Homework:
Create your unique "You Vision"

Ask yourself what do you want to *be*, *do*, and *have* relative to each facet of your retirement lifestyle. This will give you a better perspective about what is important to you and how it might manifest within your life.

For example, in the diet section of the self/health facet, list affirmations and descriptions of what you want to be in this area of your life such as *being* an "advocate of healthier eating habits." Then, in the *do* column, list what you will do as actions to achieve that. Finally, in the *have* column, list what you will enjoy or experience as a result of your actions, such as "feel healthier" or "have more energy."

What you decide to *be* in each facet of your life is your affirmation, what you want to *do* is your commitment, and what you will *have* is what you hope to experience as a result.

SELF/HEALTH FACET

To truly experience life at its fullest, it's important to feel as healthy as you are able to at each age of your life. A life-facet allocation model easily gets out of balance when we don't feel well. When the health portion of "self" enlarges due to illness, disease, or abuse, there is little room for the other, equally important facets of our lives to flourish. Likewise, if your self/health slice expands due to obsessing about working out at the gym, other important areas of your life may suffer.

There is extensive evidence linking a balance of daily diet, exercise, and rest to emotional well-being and longevity. For most people, moderation is the watchword.

Diet

Since dietary needs can vary greatly for each person, I leave it up to you to conduct your own investigation into creating and maintaining a diet that provides the right amount of good stuff to support your daily energy dietary requirements. When it comes to diet, nutritionists most often use the descriptive word "balanced."

Diet

Be (Affirm) Descriptions: Ideals/ Identities/Ideologies	Do (Commit) Specific Actions:	Have (Enjoy) Experiences:
I will Be:	I will Do:	I will Have:

Exercise

A daily exercise program is also an area that may vary depending on your personal goals and current physical condition. Always check in with your doctor before beginning or changing your exercise routine. An important element is *consistency* when it comes to physical exercise. Recent research reports that moderate exercise such as walking for forty minutes five days a week provides significant cardiovascular benefit. Bigger goals such as training for long-distance runs or triathlons should only be attempted after receiving an all clear from your health-care professional.

Exercise

Be (Affirm) Descriptions: Ideals/ Identities/Ideologies	Do (Commit) Specific Actions:	Have (Enjoy) Experiences:
I will Be:	I will Do:	I will Have:

Rest

Much has been written about the amount of rest we require based on age, stamina, and daily routine. Considering the number of sleep aids prescribed annually in the US (nine million), evidently there are a lot of people who are experiencing difficulty obtaining sufficient nighttime rest.

But it isn't just nighttime sleep we are depriving ourselves of. We also need break times throughout the day. These are little respites of time totally for you. Many people use meditation and relaxation breathing exercises to just *be* for a few minutes between daytime activities. By the way, if you are tweeting, checking email, or surfing the web during these daytime rest periods, you aren't *being;* you are *doing* and haven't given yourself the "you" time I'm describing.

Rest—Night

Be (Affirm) Descriptions: Ideals/ Identities/Ideologies	Do (Commit) Specific Actions:	Have (Enjoy) Experiences:
I will Be:	I will Do:	I will Have:

Rest—Daytime

Be (Affirm) Descriptions: Ideals/ Identities/ Ideologies	Do (Commit) Specific Actions:	Have (Enjoy) Experiences:
I will Be:	I will Do:	I will Have:

"Me" Time

Be (Affirm) Descriptions: Ideals/ Identities/ Ideologies	Do (Commit) Specific Actions:	Have (Enjoy) Experiences:
I will Be:	I will Do:	I will Have:

LIFE PARTNER

Not everyone has a life partner. If this describes you, leave an open space on your life-facet allocation model for this person, who may or may not show up in the future. Create an "ideal" list of traits for your ideal life partner. Make it a goal to become each of the ideal traits you seek in another while you are waiting.

If you do have a significant other, creating your retirement-life vision means redefining how and when you will spend time together as well as separately. What facets of your lives will you experience together, and which will you experience separately? Ideally, the plan you agree upon is mutually acceptable and open to refinement. There is no right or wrong way unless this exercise is never completed and not shared openly together.

Life Partner

Be (Affirm) Descriptions: Ideals/ Identities/ Ideologies	Do (Commit) Specific Actions:	Have (Enjoy) Experiences:
I will Be:	I will Do:	I will Have:

FAMILY/FRIENDS

What do you want to be, do, or have as you define your connection to family and friendships? What do you want to experience with each member of your family and close friends during your lifetime, especially your retirement years? What legacy are you wanting to create for these people? Remember the tombstone test?

Think of each family member and the close personal friends with whom you share relationships. Are there people in this group with whom you desire a deeper connection? Perhaps there is someone who is estranged from your life, and you wish to close the distance between you and that person. Seize the moment!

Family/Friends

Be (Affirm) Descriptions: Ideals/ Identities/ Ideologies	Do (Commit) Specific Actions:	Have (Enjoy) Experiences:
I will Be:	I will Do:	I will Have:

COMMUNITY

This facet is about leaving your footprint within the local, state, national, and international community. How much of your time, talent, and money are you willing to allocate to community service? This facet represents your contribution to humanity.

Community

Be (Affirm) Descriptions: Ideals/ Identities/ Ideologies	Do (Commit) Specific Actions:	Have (Enjoy) Experiences:
I will Be:	I will Do:	I will Have:

EXPLORE

The explore-life facet includes travel, education, recreation, and creating new experiences. This area is most often associated with what people think retirement is or will be. Usually, it is experienced more robustly earlier in retirement when vitality is at a high level.

We are never too old to stop exploring. At 104, my wife's grandmother, Grace, was still reading daily and educating herself on new topics.

Travel

Be (Affirm) Descriptions: Ideals/ Identities/ Ideologies	Do (Commit) Specific Actions:	Have (Enjoy) Experiences:
I will Be:	I will Do:	I will Have:

Education

Be (Affirm) Descriptions: Ideals/ Identities/ Ideologies	Do (Commit) Specific Actions:	Have (Enjoy) Experiences:
I will Be:	I will Do:	I will Have:

Out of the Box

Be (Affirm) Descriptions: Ideals/ Identities/ Ideologies	Do (Commit) Specific Actions:	Have (Enjoy) Experiences:
I will Be:	I will Do:	I will Have:

VOCATION/AVOCATION

During primary working years, this facet may have squeezed out other important components of your life. When the avocation facet is eliminated or shrunk down, the relevance question sometimes looms larger: How will I remain relevant when I no longer do what has defined me (my work) for so many years? Only you can answer this question. I will tell you from my own experience the answer to "how will I remain relevant in my life during retirement" question was found within and not outside myself. When I discovered that my real purpose in life had very little to do with what I did for a living, new vistas began to appear in my life. Today, I am relevant in all facets of my life—not just my vocation/avocation.

Whether paid or not, full- or part-time, continuing an active work life is closely correlated with higher levels of good health. Although some wish to trade in their vocation for a permanent vacation, others decide to continue in their current profession or an entirely new employment adventure during what are traditionally thought of as "retirement years." This last sentence describes the essence of retirement recess. Whatever you decide, remember that what you *do* and what you *have* are not the only ways of determining who you are. You are something bigger than the sum parts of all the facets of your life.

Vocation/Avocation

Be (Affirm) Descriptions: Ideals/ Identities/ Ideologies	Do (Commit) Specific Actions:	Have (Enjoy) Experiences:
I will Be:	I will Do:	I will Have:

SOMETHING BIGGER

This is my favorite life facet. It's why I'm excited to get up each morning. It's the one part of each of our lives that can't be fully defined or possessed. It is the unexplained coincidence, the inner knowing, the serendipities of life that make us smile and wonder at the same time. You can never possess the something bigger; you can only experience it.

Whether you believe in something greater or not, always leave space within your life-facet allocation for this slice to exist. Some people pursue it through religion, spirituality, meditation, or yoga. It is often most strongly felt when you are in the present moment. After a lifetime of living by the mandate of "don't just sit there; do something," it's time for a new way of *being* that includes "don't just do something; sit there."

Something Bigger

Be (Affirm) Descriptions: Ideals/ Identities/ Ideologies	Do (Commit) Specific Actions:	Have (Enjoy) Experiences:
I will Be:	I will Do:	I will Have:

After completing the previous exercises, the life-facet allocation model you create can be used as a tool to periodically compare your current lifestyle actions and behaviors to your ideal balance of time, focus, and energy in each area. Areas of your life that become out-of-balance when compared to your model allocation can be adjusted and brought back into balance much like you do with your investment plan via a life-facet-allocation rebalancing. For example, someone consumed by work (know anyone like this?) may have a vocation/avocation slice so large it squeezes the other facets into tiny slivers. The people within your family-and-friends slice will most likely attest to this. The unbalanced excess of time spent at work can be reduced and re-allocated across other life facets to bring your life back into order. This life-rebalancing action assumes, of course, that the participant wants a better balance in all aspects of life and is willing to adjust those aspects accordingly.

NEXT, TAKE THE FOLLOWING ACTIONS:

- *Important.* Make a follow-up appointment on your calendar with yourself to review your *You Vision* progress at least monthly.
- Ensure that your model allocation of time and attention to each life facet lines up with your actual allocation of time and attention to each slice of your life. If you find you are out of balance, reallocate your time and attention accordingly. Remember, you are the CEO of your life—retired or not.

DISCOVERING YOUR RELEVANCE

Your response to the *be* section of each life facet is a description of your relevance, not just in one but also in all seven areas of your life. The *do* answers detail how your actions bring new meaning in each area of your life. The *have* responses describe what you hope to experience as a result.

TAKE NOTE

REJOICE IN THE REALIZATION THAT YOUR REAL PURPOSE IS EVIDENT THROUGH ALL THE PEOPLE YOU AFFECT EACH DAY. YOU ARE RELEVANT REGARDLESS OF YOUR EMPLOYMENT STATUS.

Chapter Eight

Strategies for Moving into Retirement

N ow that you have a better idea of what you want to *be, do,* and *have* in all seven facets of your retirement life, lets discuss a couple of timing strategies to make it happen. As we think about your actual transition from work life to retirement recess, we assume the science of your retirement financial plan agrees with the timing of your decision.

For some folks, the commencement of retirement is an all-or-nothing proposition. They proclaim, "This is the date, the age, and the place." After a life of all-in, playing the employment game to support a family and personal goals, they are now cashing out and placing their chips on a gaming table called "retirement," a game most have little or no past experience in playing.

Others prefer a gradual transition from a full-time vocation to a permanent vacation. They have a written timeline and are moving closer to their full-time retirement goal over a period of months or years. Let's study both strategies more closely.

IMMEDIATE WORK TO RETIREMENT TRANSITION (ON/OFF SWITCH)

The on/off-switch strategy suits those who believe they are prepared financially and emotionally to make an immediate change from work life to retired life at a predetermined future date. Like flipping a switch, life routines are changed immediately from a schedule crammed with career responsibilities and deadlines to a retired state of mind. This strategy creates an abrupt shift to a schedule where obligations and commitments become, for the most part, self-directed rather than employer mandated. Sounds wonderful, doesn't it? As you learned earlier in the history-of-retirement section, the on/off-switch strategy has traditional roots. In the past, after reaching a certain age (usually sixty-five), most workers graduated immediately from a status of employed one day to retired the next.

An advantage of the on/off-switch approach is that it is immediate. No messing around here. These folks have no difficulty leaving their work lives far behind them—or so they hope. They are capable and willing to fill their days with activities they choose and do not suspect they will miss the social aspects and sense of belonging that their previous employment community may have provided for many years.

A disadvantage of the on/off-switch strategy is the same as the advantage—it's immediate. If it turns out that you aren't as ready financially or emotionally to retire as you initially believed, your options to reverse course (rejoin the workforce) may be limited. If your former employer has collected your building security card and replaced you or phased out your position completely, the all–or-nothing strategy could result in looking for a new employer if you discover after-the-fact that you need more employment time to better prepare for full-time retirement recess.

Caution: Those who select the on/off-switch strategy and who plan to immediately supplement monthly income with systematic distributions from investment accounts may need to plan for a unique risk called sequence-of-returns risk. This risk occurs when regular withdrawals are taken from investments coinciding with a periodic financial market decline. The result can be an unplanned accelerated spend down of investment principal if safeguards are not implemented (PCM) beforehand to mitigate this risk. Strategies to do so are discussed in chapter 12.

The immediate on-off retirement switch can be initiated by the employee (voluntary retirement) or the employer (forced retirement). Either way, this transition strategy means the adjustment period for the retiree commences immediately, whether he or she is actually prepared or not.

TRANSITIONAL WORK TO RETIREMENT (DIMMER SWITCH)

Unlike the on/off, all-or-nothing approach, a gradual, transitional strategy allows for a slower changeover from full-time employment to retirement recess for grown-ups. This approach is more like a light dimmer control than an on/off switch. It allows for additional time to gradually make the transition from a schedule dictated by employment responsibilities to one of roomier, self-directed routines. In effect, this strategy is like turning the lights slowly down on the career life you are leaving while gradually turning the lights up on the retirement lifestyle you are seeking.

TGIRF (Thank God It's Retirement Friday)!

A great idea when utilizing the transitional (dimmer switch) work-to-recess style is to practice retirement by extending the weekend to include an extra day or two each week while you still are employed. Maybe you choose to be retired every Friday at the beginning of your transition period. It's fun to tell people, "I'm retired—on Fridays." Of course, a prerequisite for this reduced work schedule is having an employer and a job description that allows for a gradual phaseout of your work commitments for your current position. If this modified work schedule is not possible within your current work environment, you may want to consider an employment or position change a couple of years prior to your ultimate retirement recess date to increase flexibility during your modified workweek. This strategy is sometimes called a "tapered" employment-to-retirement strategy.

A benefit of a gradual transition to retirement timeline is that it allows you to "practice" recess periods as you move closer to the day when the full-time recess bell rings. Preparing for a future full-time retirement by practicing it on a part-time basis will help you identify and correct potential issues ahead of time.

I like to compare this gradual transition to surfacing from a deep dive in the ocean. Unless you are wearing a pressurized suit, the ascent to the surface from below needs to be slow and steady to give the body time to adjust to the change in pressure. Think of a transitional retirement approach as a "decompression period," moving from employment pressures to retirement freedom gradually rather than abruptly. The last thing you want is a case of the "retirement bends" because you didn't allow enough time to adjust to the pressure change between full-time work and retirement recess.

Two-earner households sometimes plan for one member of the couple to begin retirement before the other. This way one of the two can test the waters before both take a plunge into the deep end of the retirement pool. Of course, it's never as much fun when half the couple is at recess and the other half is still working. This is like being on the recess playground while your best friend is still working in the classroom. Continuation of less-expensive, employer-provided group health-care insurance benefits for both the worker and the nonworking spouse is often a major reason one spouse continues working. Employer provided health insurance coverage is usually maintained until the retirees are eligible for less-expensive Medicare health insurance premiums at age sixty-five.

TAKE NOTE

IF YOU RESIGN FROM YOUR CURRENT WORK POSITION AND ACCEPT A MODIFIED (LESS-THAN-FULL-TIME) WORK ASSIGNMENT, MAKE SURE THAT YOU EVALUATE ANY LOST OR REDUCED RETIREMENT BENEFITS THAT MAY OCCUR AS A RESULT OF A CHANGE TO YOUR WORK SCHEDULE.

Assess Your Play-Ability

No matter which work-to-retirement strategy you believe is right for you—the on/off or the dimmer switch—it is important to assess your play-ability level prior to your full-time retired goal date.

What is "play-ability"? The best examples are found by observing the experts of play—children. I've never met a five-year-old who didn't know how to play with complete abandon. Children possess the ability to instinctively switch immediately from a state of idleness to play mode.

As we grow up, we devote more of our attention and time to the serious business of working for a living and dealing with the responsibilities of family life, allowing little time to practice the play skills we learned as kids. Our play abilities atrophy if they are not exercised regularly.

Do you know any grown-ups who have difficulty switching between work periods and play time? You may notice this when you begin a vacation or extended holiday. Those who have forgotten how to play have difficulty switching from full-time career to full-time retirement without a transition (decompression) period in between. The honeymoon phase of a careerless lifestyle can wear off after a short time and turn to boredom, depression, and anxiety. Alcoholism and drug addiction increase as drinks and drugs fill the void where social and status aspects of employment once resided.

Pre-cess

If practical, plan and practice playtime (minirecess) for increasing periods of time prior to your actual full-time retirement. During school years, this period was called spring or fall break and summer vacation. I call these preretirement recess periods "pre-cess." Practicing pre-cess prior to retirement recess accomplishes two important goals:

1. Emotionally, you start the process of conditioning yourself and the people around you by switching back and forth between work time and play time. This decompression step allows you time to develop your sense of balance between distinctly different routines.

2. You begin to build confidence that your current job responsibilities will allow you to break from your work routine for extended periods without the business falling apart while you are absent.

Being able to successfully delegate your work responsibilities is a skill that takes time and practice for most people to master—especially for those who have difficulty letting go.

Homework:

Schedule an extended trip to a pre-cess place (playground) you haven't visited before.

If a voice in your head says there is no way you can be gone from work even for a few days, and you are within five years of your retirement goal, you need to ask yourself the following: What significant change must occur to free me up so I can recess permanently without experiencing an emotional meltdown in the process?

YOUR PRIMARY RETIREMENT ADDRESS

Where do you want your primary residence to be located during your retirement-recess years? As you create your retirement-recess life plan, deciding on your primary, and in some cases secondary, residence is an important consideration. Some retirees choose a typical neighborhood residence—with or without provided maintenance and upkeep. Others decide to live in a home on wheels (motor home), where the view out your living room window changes as you travel. Still others decide on retirement communities catering to the traditional retirement lifestyle.

Where you decide to live during your retirement is usually based on several factors called location attractors, as described below.

- **Climate/Seasons**

  There is a difference between visiting a certain climate and living in it year-round. You may enjoy the desert heat for short periods but find it not as attractive over several months. If you prefer a change of seasons, be careful about climates where seasons don't change. Try on several possible locations for size before you commit. Also, health can be affected by climate. Give yourself enough time to fully acclimate during location-research visits before making a permanent move.

- **Geographic Proximity to Family and Friends**

  How close do you want to be to family and friends? Answers range from "next door" to "no distance is too far." While you're considering your geographic preferences, don't forget to check in with family members and close friends to better understand how they feel about the potential distance between you and them.

- **Cost of Living: General, Medical, and Insurance**

  There is a lot of information on the internet about the cost of living for just about every area in the world. Completing your homework on this "attractor" is important to your budget and your overall comfort level about the cost of living in specific areas. I'll never forget paying forty dollars for a hamburger lunch on a visit to a tropical island location. It isn't that I didn't have forty dollars. It was the principle of the thing. It darn near made a vegetarian out of me, but salads were expensive also! As it turned out, everything was expensive at this location. This extravagance was OK for a week, but personally, I wouldn't want to face resort-level expenses during my daily retirement-recess routines.

- **Social Settings and Area Amenities**

  As you complete the *be-do have* life-facet allocation assignment—*You Vision*—it will become clearer that the connection between where you choose to reside and what you decide you want to *be*, *do*, and *have* in each area of your life are closely correlated with each other. Where you live provides the backdrop for your lifestyle to play out. Answers vary. Some people enjoy solitude, and others like constant activity. Still others are attracted to a combination of quiet and crazy. This is your recess time; you get to decide which playgrounds you like the best and where you want to live in relation to them.

- **Availability of Support Facilities**

  Whether it's a club or a clinic, consider where you choose to live and what you need in terms of serving your physical, mental, emotional, and spiritual needs. Convenience is paramount. I know one retired couple that was unhappy to find out that where they chose to live did not have a service facility for their specialized antique auto. It turns out they had to drive two hundred miles to a major city to get the car serviced. Many people are choosing to retire and age at their current location (aging in place). A variety of home health-care services are available to people in their homes that can keep them from going to a facility such as an assisted living community. Research and determine if an area you are interested in calling home has the health-support services you believe you may need in the future. If you have specialized medical needs, proximity to support services becomes a very important consideration.

  If you are planning to reside out of the country for part of the year, quality medical services are an important matter when evaluating this location attractor.

- **Employment/Business Opportunities**

  As we have discussed, many retirees want to work—either for someone else or themselves—as part of their retirement recess lifestyle. If this describes you, employment opportunities within reach of where you live will be an important factor. Making sure that internet services are available is critical if you plan on communicating/working via the web. Yes, there still are places in the world where the only bars available serve nothing to quench your cell phone's need of a signal.

- **Familiarity of Location**

  This one is important. I can't tell you how many times I've heard the story of people packing up and moving to a destination they have never visited before, and once they moved there permanently, they discovered they hated it. It's wise to spend some extended time at a potential location before you call the moving company. Like an auto purchase, test-drive the location before you buy. The pre-cess assignments discussed earlier are a fun way to get your homework done in this area before you commit to a permanent location change.

- **Security**

  Do you feel reasonably safe when you visit this location? Beyond local crime reports and statistics, does this location provide a feeling of stability so that you don't worry about your safety?

Other Considerations

Will you maintain or do you maintain a primary residence and a secondary residence? If yes, describe the location, amenities, services, attractions, and activities of each residence location.

Homework:

Based on the location attractors just discussed, where do you want your primary residence to be located during your retirement-recess years?

Grading Potential Retirement Residence Locations

Location #1 Name: _____

Location #2 Name: _____

Location #3 Name: _____

Location Attractors	Location #1	Location #2	Location #3	Comments
Climate/seasons				
Geographic proximity to family and friends				
Cost of living				
Social and area amenities				
Support facilities				
Employment/business opportunities				
Familiarity of location				
Security:				
Other:				

Grading: _Ideal_ = A, _Strong_ =B, _Acceptable_ = C, _Weak_ = D, Incomplete = I

Chapter Nine

Recess Ready

The top of the class, those who have or will have their retirement planning homework finished on or before their retirement recess, are "recess ready." Want to join this group? Set a goal for yourself today to do what they do.

Who are these people? How do they do it? There really isn't a secret handshake within this crowd of people who are on the path to a fulfilling retirement recess, although they do tend to smile more often than those who aren't as prepared. Most are average folks in many respects, with a couple of very important exceptions:

1. They are and have been extremely persistent in paying themselves first each month, often devoting a high percentage (15–25 percent) of their working income, which they earmark exclusively for their future recess-play years. Not all of these savers began by earmarking 15 percent or more of their income immediately.

Many started at a lesser percentage and, after developing a savings habit, faithfully increased their contribution to their future-retirement "self" account over time.

2. They practiced the pay-self-first habit starting early in their working careers and with few exceptions never interrupted it during their entire working lifetime. Using a percentage of earnings strategy rather than a fixed dollar amount meant that as working income rose through the years, so did the actual dollar amount contributed to the chosen investment account. Recess-ready people have the discipline to focus on long-term investment results (inflation-protected income) rather than reacting to short-term market fluctuations. They took the letters a, c, t, i, o, and n from the word "procrastination" and created their own financial-independence story by leveraging time, money, and investment return. Their serious-money retirement investments work hard so one day they won't have to.

3. They allow no robbing of their serious retirement savings for impulsive purchasing or to fund requests from friends or family to open a credit line with them. They don't borrow from their retirement-savings money or tap into their home equity.

4. These retirement-ready people live within their financial means, both during working years and throughout their retirement. They are comfortable residing in the roomy middle between the two extremes of frugal and extravagant.

5. They have a vision. They know what their retirement-recess vision looks like and have a better-than-average understanding of what will be needed to make their dreams happen.

6. Finally, retirement-ready people have completed all their financial homework, either on their own or with the aid of a retirement financial adviser. They have created a plan to identify and

mitigate all seventeen specific core risks (discussed next) that can threaten their retirement income. In short, they have seized the challenge of living in the moment while planning for the future, making a commitment to go not just part way, but the entire distance to graduate at the top of the retirement-ready class.

In the next chapter, we will study the core retirement-income risks that can threaten to derail your retirement-lifestyle plan. Additionally, we will examine possible strategies available to mitigate each of them.

Chapter Ten

The Real Risk

Outliving your money is referred to as longevity risk. Longevity by itself is not the real risk you face during your retirement—unless you haven't financially prepared for it. By now most people are aware of the phenomenon of longer life spans. Living longer than previous generations affords additional time to participate and enjoy life in ways your grandparents or great-grandparents never imagined.

However, living longer during retirement does increase the number and type of potential risks associated with an early spend down of retirement savings that previous generations may not have worried about as much.

As we have discussed, recent research reveals a high percentage of people (estimates range from 50 percent to 70 percent) do not have a written financial plan. This is true despite the fact that living longer demands greater care in planning for these extended years. Of those who have a plan, many haven't taken the action to complete a comprehensive assessment designed to identify and reduce the risks that threaten an early spend down of income-generating assets. These risks can occur both before and during retirement years.

Typically, the major focus of financial planning risk-mitigation has been limited to investment management and life, disability, and medical insurance. As you will learn, planning for a longer lifetime requires evaluating additional core risks to better ensure an uninterrupted stream of income throughout your retirement recess.

A FEAR GREATER THAN DYING

As a society, we don't like to think or talk much about the one event that will occur with 100 percent certainty for every human on the planet—dying. Even though most of us fear death at some level, there exists a fear greater than dying. It's the fear of running out of money before running out of lifetime and becoming financially dependent on others.

I've never met anyone who isn't worried about the prospects of becoming financially dependent on family or others sometime during their lifetimes. Even the ultrawealthy express fears of losing all their wealth before the end of their lives. No one wants to be a burden, especially to family, at any point in their lives—most certainly not in their later years.

Failure to identify and manage the core financial, economic, and personal risks (intensified by longer retirement periods) *is* the real risk. The anticipation and actual experience of an early asset spend down is devastating, and most people admit they fear financial dependence on others more than death itself.

Chapter Eleven

Risk—Cause and Effect

Living your dream while maintaining lifelong financial freedom is the ultimate goal of comprehensive retirement financial planning. Identifying causes that threaten the ability to remain financially free is significantly important to achieving and maintaining this goal.

All risks are driven by one or more events that can happen independently from one another or simultaneously with one another. Some risk causes can be anticipated in advance, and others surprise us quite unexpectedly. We all experience events during our lives that are within our control to manage and some that simply are not. Managing those risks within the realm of our control is the focus of our next exercise.

If a triggering risk event does not occur, no actual harm results, except maybe worry wrinkles. For example, if you haven't done your estate homework and written a will, created a trust (if applicable), and purchased life insurance (if the financial need is present), and the triggering event (death) hasn't occurred yet, the associated damaging consequences of not completing your estate homework before your unexpected demise will not impact your survivors. In essence, "you get away with it."

For the financial-risk events that do occur at some point, how we initially react, especially to events that surprise us, will often determine the magnitude of damage created. Pausing before responding, especially if your normal reaction tends to be charged with, shall we say, strong emotion, can make a huge difference in the scale of damage resulting both from the triggering event and any collateral damage caused by an emotional outbreak. Panic selling of investments during a normal periodic market decline often turns a temporary downturn in financial market values (that historically have a high likelihood of recovering value) into an irreversible loss. A professional "calm voice of reason" resource positioned between the reactor and the event can prove to be an important buffer to your financial and emotional well-being— especially if you are prone to be a worrier and/or an overreactor. By the way, if you haven't figured it out yet, the mainstream media are not a good "calm voice of reason." In fact, because the mania media always reports any and all news as "breaking," saturated in emotional innuendos, most people need a "centering" source of reason to get regrounded after subjecting themselves to the hysteria hour that is called the evening news.

To illustrate, meet Bob and Alice. Wanting to create an inflation-protected income stream for their retirement-recess years, the newly retired couple do their research and invest part of their retirement assets in a professionally managed diversified investment portfolio containing inflation-fighting, dividend-paying stocks of well-managed, high-quality companies. It sounds sensible, doesn't it? It is, right up to the point when a sudden periodic decline in the financial markets (cause by a triggering event) causes a sizable drop in the value of Bob and

Alice's retirement account. In the absence of being reminded to focus on long-term permanent goals and not short-term temporary events, they believe (with the full support of the financial news hour) that this is a permanent rather than temporary setback. In other words—once again the world is ending. The fearful couple immediately overreacts; they call the customer service number for their investment account and request an immediate sale of all shares during the decline; this "effect" locks in what may have been a temporary decline as a permanent financial loss. These folks have become "ready, fire, aim" reactors rather than methodical responders. But wait, it gets worse. After selling at a loss, they then gather the remains of their retirement account carnage and deposit it in a near-zero-interest-earning money market account. So much for protecting future income from inflationary increases.

There is no guarantee that periodic financial market drops that cause resulting declines in your investment account will ever lead to recovered declines over time. However, selling shares during financial market values via an emotional panic converts what may have been a temporary loss to an almost certain, dare I say guaranteed, permanent loss. It would have been better if Bob and Alice had preplanned (PCM) for periodic financial market volatility by seeking competent financial education about the normalcy of such events; created an alternative income plan for these inevitable periods; and found a "calm voice of reason" to reassure them that perhaps the world wasn't ending (if it were, none of this would matter). Then things may have turned out differently.

TAKE NOTE

EVERYONE NEEDS A SOURCE OF CALM REASON IN A WORLD OF HYPED, TWENTY-FOUR-HOUR BREAKING NEWS. IF YOUR SERENITY IS IN SHORT SUPPLY, CONSIDER DELEGATING INVESTMENT DISCIPLINE TO A PROFESSIONAL WHO HAS EXCESS CALM REASONING TO SHARE WITH YOU.

Chapter Twelve

Retirement Income Security Killers (RISK)

I t's not realistic to expect that a riskless life is possible, especially when it comes to retirement planning. As with life itself, there are risks that threaten to derail even the best-formed financial plans. I call those threats to your retirement-income security, which need to be identified *before* (not *after*) they take effect, retirement income security killers, or RISK.

The goal of a retirement-income risk-management assessment is not to do the impossible—eliminate all risks. What is possible is to assess your situation and prioritize each potential RISK as high, medium, or low impact and choose an appropriate strategy to mitigate those risks in order of impact priority, beginning with the highest potential RISK first.

COMPREHENSIVE RISK MANAGEMENT IS ACCOMPLISHED IN FOUR PLANNING STEPS:

1. **Identify and define** each core RISK.
2. **Evaluate** the probability and impact of a specific RISK affecting your plan now or in the future.
3. **Choose and implement** one of the four RISK-mitigation strategies: ignore, assume, avoid, or transfer.
4. **Monitor** the plan for potential new RISKs not present during the last assessment.

STEP ONE: IDENTIFY AND DEFINE THE CORE RISK

Planning for a historically long retirement recess requires looking beyond traditional retirement planning methods to ready ourselves for a successful retirement recess. The longer you plan to go, the more you need to know about the hazards that can impede financial independence along the way.

There are seventeen core risks, within three RISK categories, that everyone who aspires to one day ring the retirement-recess bell should study. Left unchecked, these impediments to retirement income have the power to transport you—sometimes quickly, sometimes slowly—from a sunny place of financial freedom to the dark caverns of your adult children's basement—providing of course that your adult children are still not living in your basement.

It is not likely that your present situation will be subject to all seventeen core risks simultaneously, at least let's hope not. However, everyone is susceptible to some core risks at different stages of his or her life.

The three main RISK categories are investment/financial, economic, and personal. Within each of these main categories are the core risks detailed below.

Investment/Financial RISK

    Single-investment risk

    Periodic financial market value fluctuation risk, aka market risk

    Sequence-of-investment-return risk

    Excess-withdrawal risk

    Asset-allocation risk

    Liquidity risk

Economic RISK

    Inflation risk

    Interest-rate risk

    Tax-cost risk

    Financial-strength risk

Personal-Event RISK

    Entitlement-income risk

    Uninsured medical risk

    Lifestyle risk

    Life happens risk

    Employment risk

    Media risk

    Procrastination risk (no coincidence this one is last)

CORE-RISK DEFINITIONS

Investment/Financial RISK Group

Single-Investment Risk: Type 1: The risk of a potential or actual permanent loss of invested money in a single, nondiversified investment company or entity. Type 2: The risk that investment future value is insufficient to satisfy an investment objective.

Possible Causes of Single-Investment Risk
- Lack of broad-based diversification
- Speculation
- Poor company/investment management/no (or limited) company financial/market history
- Fraud
- Insufficient investment holding period and lack of investment discipline
- Investment performance adversely and sometimes permanently affected by political/economic/financial/geopolitical and other developments not always predictable and/or avoidable

Possible Single-Investment Risk-Mitigation Strategies
- Diversification—owning many, not just a few, securities differentiated by industry, size, country, and market within an investment account.
- Professional research/management—third-party delegation of asset investigation, timing of purchase, sale, and ongoing management (active management)
- Creating and following a written investment policy

GOOD TO KNOW

All investments carry some degree of risk. Investment in stocks, property, or other ventures is done for the hope of gain but with the potential risk of loss. An investment in a single financial security such as a stock or bond has a higher risk of potential permanent loss than a diversified portfolio of securities managed over time.

When a single investment is part of an overall diversified investment portfolio containing many securities, the risk of loss is still present, but diminished when the losing, single investment loss is a fraction of the portfolio rather than 100 percent of the investment account.

> ***Periodic Financial-Market Value-Fluctuation Risk***—The risk caused by the moment-by-moment price change of a financial asset due to many different circumstances. The most frequent circumstance cited is an increase in uncertainty levels affecting financial markets. Negative price volatility increases the risk of an emotional sell-off of the asset by the owner at a value lower than the purchase price or less than the investment goal.

Possible Causes of Periodic Financial-Market Value-Fluctuation Risk

- Selling investments during periodic financial-market fluctuation at a value lower than the purchase price
- Believing periodic financial-market value-fluctuation risk is investment risk
- Insufficient research/education in investment strategies
- Being overly influenced by others, especially the broadcast media, during periods of heightened market volatility and uncertainty
- Making unsuitable investment choice(s) for one's emotional temperament
- Investment decision based on too much greed or fear
- Lack of available (liquid) stable-value money sources (cash reserves) for usage during periodic financial declines in the financial markets
- Investment objective based on current performance only and not long-term potential value (playing the market)

Possible Risk-Mitigation Solutions for Periodic Financial-Market Value-Fluctuation Risk

- Accept that periodic financial-market value fluctuations are normal.

- Don't sell shares of investments affected by periodic financial-market value volatility during heightened negative-value periods (discipline).
- Periodically rebalance asset-allocation percentages.
- Complete an annual investor temperament questionnaire and match investment allocation accordingly.
- Employ a strategy that includes long-term investing discipline—or delegate decisions to a professional money manager who possesses this discipline (calm voice of reason).
- Establish and adequately fund a ready cash (crash) reserve and utilize it during periodic financial-market declines.
- Adopt an investment policy that includes a strategy to harvest (redeem profitable shares) for future money needs during profitable periods. Buy and hold additional shares when appropriate during declining market periods.
- Conduct or hire unbiased, independent investment research.

GOOD TO KNOW

Market volatility occurs every day in different segments of the financial markets worldwide. Stock market price volatility is a measurement describing the up and down value changes of a company, industry, or the stock market in general at a given moment in time.

Financial market volatility by itself is not risk. Not everyone who owns stocks experiences a permanent loss during periods of intensified financial-market volatility. Only those who sell during such declines create permanent loss. A paper loss is not necessarily permanent until the shares are sold at a value less than the purchase price or for an amount less than expected.

Consider the following:

- Periodic stock market price volatility can be caused by an unlimited variety of real and/or imagined conditions that are usually the result of heightened uncertainty. Periodic financial-market price volatility provides both uncertainty and opportunity at the same time, depending on your attitude, goals, and objectives.
- Stock market price volatility represents both declining and advancing value periods. However, declining periods receive nearly all the media headline attention.
- Financial-market volatility can be reduced but not eliminated through investment-class diversification (owning different asset classes not directly correlated with one another, such as stocks, bonds, real estate, and metals.) Although asset diversification can minimize negative volatility (market loss), it also minimizes positive volatility (market gain).
- The risk from financial-market volatility is not from the value fluctuation itself. Rather, it is from investors selling shares during such periods, resulting in a value less than what's been invested or less than what's anticipated.

TAKE NOTE

INVESTOR TIP: IF YOU WANT TO REDUCE THE VOLATILITY OF A WELL-MANAGED, DIVERSIFIED PORTFOLIO OF STOCKS, REDUCE THE NUMBER OF TIMES YOU CHECK ITS VALUE EACH DAY.

> *Sequence-of-Investment-Return Risk*—The risk of systematic withdrawal of a fixed amount of money from a variable (fluctuating value) investment affected and coinciding with a periodic financial-market value decline. This is especially impactful if occurring near the beginning of a distribution period.

Possible Causes of Sequence-of-Investment-Return Risk

- Relying on misleading average-investment-return assumptions rather than actual year-by-year total-return investment performance when constructing a retirement-income investment plan.
- Assuming variable investment returns will not be negative during early years of a systematic distribution period, also known as the "I feel lucky syndrome"
- Lack of available alternative income sources such as cash reserves or a standby equity or reverse mortgage credit line during years of negative investment return
- Lack of budget flexibility to reduce spending and investment distributions during negative performance periods

Possible Risk-Mitigation Strategies for Sequence-of-Investment-Return Risk

- As a component of financial planning, hypothetically put to a stress test planned withdrawals from your investment portfolio prior to implementation by simulating several different long-term investment periods, including a variety of both strong and weak market periods. Adjust your distribution plan accordingly.
- Stop or reduce income withdrawals during extended declining-value periods. Establish a stable-value cash reserve to supplement income during negative-market periods. Consider building up three to five years of income reserve prior to implementing

an income distribution program. Replenish this reserve during positive-value (strong market performance) years. Examples of stable-value cash reserves are as follows: money market account, high yield savings account, reverse mortgage, or home equity line of credit.

- Establish a flexible income-distribution plan where income is reduced in negative-earning years and increased during positive-earning years.
- Consider creating retirement income from guaranteed-income sources:
- Utilize guaranteed withdrawal benefit (GWB) riders added to a low-cost variable-annuity program. (Yes, low-cost variable annuities do exist. Those who report otherwise are suffering from biased-research syndrome).
- Start a guaranteed immediate annuity payout. Usually more favorable payouts are experienced at older ages (age seventy-five-plus) and during periods when high interest rates are prevalent.
- Create bond laddering, in which bond maturities are staggered over many years. Make sure your bond ladder is leaning against a wall earning positive real returns. Real returns equal interest yield minus inflation.
- Consider a reverse mortgage line of credit amount if appropriate for your situation. Requirements are that you be age sixty-two or older, have equity in your primary residence, and have a desire to remain in the home.

EXTRA CREDIT

GO TO WWW.RETIREMENTRECESS.COM/RETIRE-READY-RESOURCE-CENTER
AND STUDY THE EXAMPLE OF SEQUENCE-OF-RETURN EFFECT ON PRINCIPAL.
THE EXAMPLE IS TITLED REVERSAL OF FORTUNE.

GOOD TO KNOW

Although a random order of positive and negative investment returns occurs within the financial markets all the time, the risk of a premature spend down of principal increases if the sequence of investment returns includes negative returns *and* systematic distributions at the same time.

Utilizing a distribution plan of fixed monthly payments during periodic financial market declines, especially in the early years of distribution, can accelerate a spend down of principle even when the historic average return percentage is higher than the actual withdrawal percentage. The effect of this phenomenon is quite different when investing money (accumulation phase) during a declining financial market, when each investment actually buys additional shares when those shares drop in price.

> **Excess-Withdrawal-Amount Risk**—The risk of withdrawing a fixed, systematic, or lump-sum amount of money as a percentage of account value that is greater than the investment's current ability to sustain its principal value over time.

Possible Causes for Excess-Withdrawal-Amount Risk

- The initial income distribution amount is too high based on the time period (term) of expected distributions and the actual investment performance over that period
- The demand for distribution exceeds expected future earning capability of investment to sufficiently replace the amount of withdrawal.
- There is a failure to adjust the income-distribution amount when the account value declines due to periodic market fluctuations, resulting in the distribution percentage rising to an excessive amount.
- The lack of emergency cash reserves forces excess withdrawals from an investment account to pay costs of emergencies.

Possible Risk-Mitigation Strategy for Excess-Withdrawal-Amount Risk

- Plan for and utilize a conservative (lower) withdrawal amount from variable investments when possible. The lower the percentage of distribution, the higher the probability of success.
- Don't rely on rules of thumb—generalizations of a "safe" withdrawal percentage for your specific income situation. Determine what is reasonable for you and your situation. Seek professional help.
- Consider establishing guaranteed annuity payments with an inflation rider included. Note: This strategy may increase

liquidity risk (ability to access principal investment). A liquidity rider can be added at an additional expense to reduce this risk.

- Establish and maintain a cash reserve to cover unexpected emergency costs.

GOOD TO KNOW

Retirement-income planning researchers have often tried without success to define the ultimate long-term "safe" withdrawal percentage rate from a retirement account. In these studies, "safe" is defined as a percentage of withdrawal with a high level of confidence that the amount will not cause the principal investment to be depleted. Hypothetical investment periods for these studies usually span a retirement lifetime of several decades.

To determine the safe withdrawal percentage rate, hypothetical withdrawal percentages are subjected to stress testing using a computer program called Monte Carlo simulation. This program subjects a assumed investment and distribution amount to thousands of random historic investment scenarios and analyzes the data. The result provides a confidence level expressed as a percentage that a given investment allocation and distribution percentage will or will not be depleted over a retirement lifetime. Investment simulation results do not guarantee actual results and are subject to other factors that may distort results. More on this topic later.

> **Asset-Allocation Risk**
>
> Type 1: The risk that the investment strategy is too conservative or too aggressive for the planned time-to-goal period
>
> Type 2: The risk that there is inadequate diversification among investments and asset classes, with securities holdings that are too concentrated—for example, in company stock
>
> Type 3: The risk of owning several different investment names that all have the same investment objective

Possible Causes for Asset-Allocation Risk

- Lack of specific long-term planning goals
- Insufficient investor long-term discipline
- Investment allocation based on emotions of fear or greed; investment plan not linked to financial goals but rather to chasing short-term performance or fearing the next market crash
- Lack of professional management of both the investment and the investor

Possible Risk-Mitigation Strategies for Asset-Allocation Risk

- Establish a suitable investment allocation for time-to-goal objectives.
- Maintain and adhere to a written investment policy and update it annually.
- Maintain or delegate investment discipline. Hire professional management.
- Rebalance investment allocation periodically—at least annually.

GOOD TO KNOW

Imagine asset allocation as a basket of fruit. The basket is your account registration type—such as an IRA or 401(k)—and the varieties of fruit within each basket are the individual investment holdings (stocks, bonds, cash, real estate, commodities, and so on). Depending on your preference for investment management, each investment can be held in the form of an individual security, a managed mutual fund, a real estate investment trust (REIT), or an exchange traded fund (ETF). For example, a common stock can be held in an IRA or 401(k) account as an individual holding or as part of a managed mutual fund that includes hundreds of other stocks. Or it can be held as an index of stocks in a fund that holds stocks of a specific index or slice of the overall market. Bonds can be held the same way—individually, through a mutual fund holding other bonds, or through an "index bond fund" holding bonds of a specific index of the bond market as a whole.

The account registration (basket) determines the distribution tax rules and tax treatment of the account. A traditional IRA, funded with tax-deductible contributions, is tax-deferred until distributions are taken at a later date, when it is subject to certain tax rules. It can hold any of the above-mentioned securities (fruit). Think of an IRA as the basket and not the fruit. In other words, an IRA is an account registration, not a specific investment. An IRA basket, by the nature of its registration, is tax-deferred or tax-free if you use the Roth type of IRA. You are likely to own several baskets (registrations) that make up your total retirement investment inventory. Examples of retirement investment baskets might include a traditional IRA, a Roth IRA, a 401(k), a tax-deferred annuity, cash-value life insurance, and taxable investment accounts.

To reduce concentrated risk, you want your retirement investment basket(s) to include many kinds of fruit rather than just one or a few choices. Lack of diversification can increase risk as you become too dependent on one class of investments. Using the fruit example, what if your basket contained only oranges, and something negative happened to orange crops? The impact of the risk would not be as high if your oranges were part of a wider fruit selection rather than being the only fruit in the basket.

Another type of diversification risk is thinking you are well diversified because you own several different investments in your account, but upon closer examination, you really own several different investment names that invest in the same things. When novice participants choose their diversification among many fund choices, as with a 401(k), they often select several funds with the best recent performance. When a particular asset class has performed well recently, all fund choices with the same investment objective would most likely have performed well. A well-diversified investment portfolio will have investments within the basket that aren't performing the same over a given period. Remember—not all fruit is in season at the same time.

> **_Liquidity Risk_**—The risk of the inability to redeem or liquidate all or a portion of an investment when needed or required without substantial penalty costs and/or loss of principal.

Possible Causes of Liquidity Risk

- Investing in programs with set maturity dates that do not match the liquidity date (when the money is needed) without paying an early withdrawal penalty
- Lack of liquid accounts reserved for short-term goals and emergencies

Possible Risk-Mitigation Strategies for Liquidity Risk

- If you own investments with maturity dates, stagger (ladder) the maturity dates.
- Establish and maintain sufficient liquid cash reserves for short-term goals and emergencies.

GOOD TO KNOW

Bonds, certificates of deposit, annuities, limited partnerships, and investment trusts are examples of investments with maturity dates for which a penalty cost may be incurred if a partial or full redemption is made prior to the maturity date. Maturity dates vary at issue. The cost of higher liquidity is the relatively low interest rate received that historically underperforms cost-of-living increases. The cost of nonsufficient liquidity reserves can be much higher.

ECONOMIC RISK GROUP

Inflation Risk—The risk of the rising cost of essential and non-essential living expenses outpacing investment earnings or income over time. Inflation results in future decreased purchasing power.

Possible Causes for Inflation Risk
- Lack of adequate planning for future cost-of-living increases
- Income sources concentrated in low-interest and/or fixed-income investments that historically do not keep up with inflationary increases
- Overdependence on future cost-of-living increases from Social Security and pension plans that historically trail actual cost-of-living increases

Possible Risk-Mitigation Strategy for Inflation Risk
- Diversify the investment allocation to include inflation-protected investments such as growth stocks, treasury inflation-protected securities (TIPS), common stock dividends, real estate, precious metals, and inflation-adjusted annuities.

USING A HISTORIC INFLATION ASSUMPTION, THE COST OF LIVING WILL DOUBLE ABOUT EVERY TWENTY-FIVE YEARS. SOME COSTS, SUCH AS MEDICAL EXPENSES, WILL HISTORICALLY DOUBLE EVEN SOONER.

GOOD TO KNOW

Retirement spending behavior reveals that retirees are more susceptible to inflationary pressures in the first ten to fifteen years of retirement than later on. The reason: There's a more active lifestyle as retirement begins, demanding greater spending early on versus an increased sedentary lifestyle resulting in reduced spending patterns in later years. Think of the early satges of retirement lifestyle as the "retirement puberty phase." The retirement hormones kick in during this most-active living phase of retirement recess, and they decrease as your retirement life ages.

Some expenses will increase faster than others during a retirement lifetime. Leading the list of inflatables are health-care costs. Between 2000 and 2009, health-care costs rose 149 percent, according to a Willis Towers Watson health-care survey. For a retired couple, it is estimated that one out of every five dollars (20 percent) spent each month on expenses goes toward health care. Rising health-care costs are the second-largest expense in retirement (after housing), according to the Urban Institute.

> ***Interest Rate Risk***—The risk that falling interest rates reduce future interest/dividend income amounts and increase reinvestment risk if invested into lower-interest-rate bonds. Rising interest rates impact bond market values negatively prior to their maturity dates. The longer the bond maturity at issue, the greater the potential decline in value prior to maturity as interest rates rise.

Possible Causes for Interest-Rate Risk

- Lack of asset diversification
- Overdependence on interest-rate-sensitive investments for retirement income

Possible Risk-Mitigation Strategies for Interest-Rate Risk

- Extend bond and certificate of deposit maturities out prior to periods of falling interest rates. Reduce bond maturities when interest rates are rising.
- If the stability of bond principal value is important, reduce bond maturities during periods of rising rates and accept lower annual yields.

GOOD TO KNOW

Real interest rates are determined by subtracting the rate of inflation from the interest yield to get the net real purchasing power, or the after-inflation rate of return. Interest rate yields can be deceiving when compared to purchasing power. For example, in the year 1980, the interest rate on a bank six-month certificate of deposit (CD) averaged 12.5 percent nationally. Wow, what people would give for that rate today. Yet the cost-of-living increase (inflation) in 1980 was 13.5 percent! This difference resulted in a real interest rate of return, or purchasing power rate, of negative 1 percent. This means the holder of this CD actually was losing money in terms of increased purchasing power when comparing the 12.5 percent rate of return and the 13.5 percent rate of inflation. Conversely, in 2016 a six-month CD earned 0.14 percent (that's zero point one four percent, not fourteen percent). When we subtract the inflation rate for 2016, 1.2 percent, from the interest rate, we end up with a real interest rate return of negative 1.06 percent, or about the same as 1980. If you want to get even more depressed, subtract federal and state taxes from the 0.14 percent interest earnings and the real rate of return is even less. The conclusion from this example—regardless of CD interest rates (13.5 percent or 0.14 percent), is that neither one kept pace with the rising cost of living.

Remember, it's not what you earn that is important. What's critical is what you can purchase with what you keep. To wit, interest-bearing accounts historically do not keep pace with cost-of-living increases over the long-term. To stay even with future inflation increases based on current inflation rates (2018) and income tax costs, most long-term investors will need to average a minimum of 5 percent per year on their investment accounts.

> **Tax-Cost Risk**—Type 1: The risk of rising or unplanned tax expense. Type 2: The risk of lack of knowledge regarding income tax saving and asset-distribution strategies—paying more than the required amount of income taxes.

Possible Causes for Tax-Cost Risk

- Tax law ignorance—especially concerning tax laws related to retirement-planning strategies
- Lack of proactive tax-planning advice
- Investment plan is overconcentrated in tax-deferred accounts versus taxable and tax-free accounts
- Accounting errors and/or omissions

Possible Risk-Mitigation Strategy for Tax-Cost Risk

- Learn and know the tax law advantages and disadvantages for your unique retirement situation.
- Seek competent annual tax return preparation *and* active tax-strategy planning. The former involves filing your annual tax return accurately; the latter involves income tax saving strategies like investing on a before-tax basis, deferring taxable earnings you are not spending now, optimizing the timing of the sale of appreciated assets, and searching for additional allowable deductions. These two activities—income tax preparation and tax planning—are not always completed by the same professional.

GOOD TO KNOW

In 2016, Americans paid $3.3 trillion in federal taxes and $1.6 trillion in state and local taxes, for a total bill of almost $5.0 trillion, or 31 percent of the nation's income. That same year, Americans collectively spent more on taxes than on food, clothing, and housing combined.

It's never been more important for all taxpaying citizens to mini-mize income tax cost and pay only the legally required amount. Unfortunately, the IRS doesn't send helpful-hints messages if you didn't realize you qualified for additional deductions that might lower your tax liability. Adjustments can be made on an amended return but only if you or someone else is aware of them. However, the IRS does send notices of adjusted taxes if it spots an error on your return.

Many people find it beneficial to consider converting a portion of tax-deferred assets from a traditional IRA or 401(k) into a tax-free Roth IRA during low-income years. For example, if you are unemployed during a year, it may be a good opportunity to consider converting a portion of tax-deferred investments from an IRA to a Roth IRA if your marginal tax bracket has dropped considerably due to reduced working income. Also, new studies suggest that the old rule of thumb about the traditional order of asset distribution in retirement may not be the most tax-efficient order compared to hybrid-distribution strate-gies. Depending on personal goals and needs, consider a balanced approach to redeeming assets over time rather than the more common approach of liquidating one asset class at a time.

TAKE NOTE

I DON'T MIND PAYING MY FAIR SHARE IN TAXES.
I JUST DON'T WANT TO BE GIVING A HUGE TIP TO THE IRS.

Financial-Strength Risk—The risk of owning or affiliating with a company or entity experiencing difficulty in honoring its obligations to pay claims, principal, income, or dividends.

Possible Causes for Financial-Strength Risk

- Owning or affiliating with companies without researching their financial stability before hand
- Lack of diversification
- No or insufficient regular review of the investment company or entity
- Ownership of companies, either directly or indirectly, with substandard financial conditions or weak credit ratings

Possible Risk-Mitigation Strategies for Financial-Strength Risk

- Engage a third-party firm to provide unbiased research.
- Perform an active review during changing financial conditions.
- Use only highly rated companies within investment and insurance plans.
- Diversify. If one shiny apple goes bad, you have other fruit to consume.

GOOD TO KNOW

The ability for a company to honor its claims is contingent on the company's financial health. In particular, an insurance company's financial strength can be evaluated by researching it through several independent companies that rate insurance companies. They are Weiss, A.M. Best, Fitch, Standard & Poor's, and Moody's.

PERSONAL/PLANNING EVENT RISK GROUP

> ***Income-Entitlement Risk***—Type 1: The risk of being overly dependent on Social Security and/or pension income benefits. Type 2: The risk of lack of knowledge regarding Social Security and pension income maximization strategies prior to irrevocable elections of benefit amounts.

Possible Causes for Income-Entitlement Risk
- Lack of comprehensive retirement-income planning
- Procrastination
- Insufficient investment-income sources to fund lifestyle goals in addition to expected entitlement-income sources

Possible Risk-Mitigation strategy for Income-Entitlement Risk
- Complete a Social Security and/or pension-income maximization exercise to determine optimal timing for each of these income sources.
- Create non-entitlement retirement-income sources (investments, real estate, business) in addition to entitlement-income sources such as Social Security and/or pensions.

GOOD TO KNOW

People become overly dependent on Social Security and/or pension benefits by default. When no other source of retirement income is created during working years, entitlement-income dependency risk increases. As we have discussed, Social Security and pension benefits alone were never meant to be the sole sources of retirement income. The average Social Security benefit check in 2016 was $1,341 per month. That's hardly enough to live on by itself, yet in 2016, 23 percent of married couples and about 43 percent of unmarried persons relied on Social Security for 90 percent or more of their income.

> ***Uninsured Medical Risk***—Type1: The risk of substandard or no medical insurance coverage. Type 2: The risk of insufficient cash reserves to cover out-of-pocket medical and extraordinary expenses when they occur.

Possible Causes for Uninsured Medical Risk

- Lack of knowledge regarding uninsured medical costs and limitations of current insurance coverage
- Inability to obtain affordable insurance coverage due to age and/or health
- Unwillingness to transfer the financial risk of medical expense to an insurance carrier prior to occurrence
- Insufficient or wrong type of coverage—lack of comprehensive medical coverage
- Falsely believing Medicare will cover all long-term health-care costs

Possible Risk-Mitigation Strategy for Uninsured Medical Risk

- Thoroughly review all medical insurance coverages on an annual basis and close coverage gaps when possible.

GOOD TO KNOW

According to a health-care white paper, Fidelity estimates that a sixty-five-year-old couple that retired in 2009 would need to have saved approximately $240,000 to $415,000 to cover medical costs in retirement. An updated review in 2015 revealed an average retirement medical-cost estimate of $245,000 on the low end. This figure could be much higher if one or both spouses developed a degenerative illness such as Alzheimer's disease. These estimates do not include other health-related expenses such as over-the-counter medications, most dental services, and long-term care expenses.

EXTRA CREDIT

EXTRA CREDIT

EXTRA CREDIT

GO TO WWW.RETIREMENTRECESS.COM/RETIRE-READY-RESOURCE-CENTER AND ACCESS LONG-TERM CARE COSTS—MEDICARE COSTS AND TRENDS. ALSO READ: WHAT THE INSURANCE INDUSTRY DOESN'T TELL YOU ABOUT PRESCRIPTION DRUG COSTS.

Lifestyle Risk: Type 1: The risk of insufficient income to sustain a desired lifestyle during retirement years—or attempting to live a champagne lifestyle funded by a beer budget. Type 2: The risk of living on limited fixed income, resulting in a lifestyle that causes retirement discontent.

Possible Causes for Lifestyle Risk
- Lacking in knowledge and planning and failing to compute adequate amounts and/or computing erroneous amounts of savings required to fully fund an expected lifestyle goal
- Funding adult children's living expenses with retirement assets
- Procrastinating—not saving for retirement income years earlier, when goals are more achievable, otherwise known as the "I thought I had time" syndrome
- Overestimating income potential of investments or understating expected expenses during retirement (lack of formal retirement financial planning)
- Carrying too much debt into retirement, requiring increased income from limited resources to make minimum debt payments

Possible Risk-Mitigation Strategies for Lifestyle Risk
- Complete a comprehensive financial plan, including a life-planning exercise.
- Begin planning and saving early for retirement years.
- Perform accurate and inclusive budget exercises. Specifically, create a budget that breaks down monthly cash flow expenses into two categories: Essentials (your must-have expenses) and nonessentials (your wants and wishes).
- Maintain disciplined spending within financial means.
- Have the "talk" with financially dependent adult children and

set their "launch date."

- Create a plan to eliminate all major debts prior to retirement.

GOOD TO KNOW

Depending on what group you ask, between 50 and 80 percent of those surveyed have no idea how much money they will need by the time they ring the recess bell. Of those who do know, serious doubts arise about how best to actually save that amount and then how to manage the needed distributions over an extended retirement.

Determining your retirement-savings goal is the first step in the process of becoming financially independent. The ideal age to begin the process of answering the "how much money will be enough" question is as young as possible. Unfortunately, by the time most people begin to seriously seek an answer, they have lost valuable time, making the attainment of this goal much harder to accomplish. If you haven't sought an answer yet, begin today.

Life Happens Risk—The risk of an unexpected or unplanned change in personal or family circumstances, such as death, accident, disability, illness, injury, marital status revision, employment alteration, lawsuit, or fraud. This includes the incapacity risk of being unable to personally manage your own financial affairs.

Possible Causes for Life Happens Risk

- Lack of planning for life's circumstances
- Being uninsured, underinsured, uninsurable, or owning the wrong type of insurance
- No written will, power of attorney, or medical directives

Possible Risk-Mitigation Strategies for Life Happens Risk

- Schedule comprehensive and periodic insurance coverage reviews.
- Maintain a written financial plan with wills, power of attorney, medical power of attorney, and, if applicable, a trust. Review beneficiaries and payable-upon-death registrations annually.
- Sign a prenuptial or postnuptial agreement, if appropriate.
- Establish and maintain an emergency cash reserve.
- Sign up for disability income insurance, if applicable.
- Maintain an umbrella liability insurance policy.
- Implement a personal identification information (PII) protection program.
- Secure sufficient auto, homeowners, and property-hazard insurance. Review coverage annually.

GOOD TO KNOW

Too often we hear or read stories about someone who has suffered a personal financial loss. In almost all cases, the financial crisis created as a result of the loss could have been reduced by proactively planning ahead rather hoping it wouldn't happen. John Lennon was right—"Life is what happens while we are making other plans." Mitigate the risks for the "life happens" events.

> **Employment Risk**—The risk of unexpected loss of employment income due to circumstances beyond your control such as changing health (yours or that of a family member) or labor market supply and demand changes.

Possible Causes for Employment Risk

- Being overly dependent on employment income during later years due to lack of planning, savings, and procrastination
- Having lack of sufficient nonemployment income sources—see above

Possible Risk-Mitigation Strategies for Employment Risk

- Create a plan to limit dependence on postretirement employment income.
- Form an available investment pool to supplement income when employment ends.
- Establish a goal to begin retirement recess when available income sources can fund retirement expenses without the need of employment income.
- Complete a retirement-recess monthly lifestyle expense budget. Match essential expenses with guaranteed-income resources like Social Security, pension, and annuity payments. Pay for nonessential expenses with employment income and retirement savings accounts.

GOOD TO KNOW

There is an increasing trend toward delaying full retirement by continuing to work until a later age. Living longer is creating a need for many people to consider a full-retirement age beyond the traditional age of sixty-five. Extended employment buys additional years to catch up on retirement contributions, allow retirement investments to grow, and it reduces the years these investments must provide an income substitute. Continued employment also allows for a delay in filing for Social Security or pension-income benefits, which can result in a larger benefit when you do decide it's time to collect. However, relying solely on employment income for retirement expenses as we age comes with a high risk when employment terminates. Who or what will replace lost wages when the job ends?

EMPLOYMENT RISK IS PRESENT THROUGHOUT AN ENTIRE WORKING CAREER. IT INCREASES WHEN REEMPLOYMENT BECOMES HARDER TO ACCOMPLISH DUE TO CHANGING HEALTH CONDITIONS AND EMPLOYMENT TRENDS.

Media Risk—Type 1: The risk of being overly influenced by mainstream media hype. Type 2: The risk of acting on specific financial advice given by people in the media (including financial adviser radio talk shows and blogs) who freely offer specific investment advice but know nothing about your unique circumstances.

Possible Causes for Media Risk

- Lack of unbiased, independent, professional guidance
- Investing by emotion only
- Taking financial advice from people you don't know and from those who don't know you

Possible Risk-Mitigation Strategies for Media Risk

- Only act on financial advice given to you by someone (a professional) who knows you and your circumstances.
- Filter all mainstream media hype through the calm voice of reason provided by a third-party financial adviser who is familiar with your goals and temperament.

GOOD TO KNOW

Some of the specific recommendations made through a book, blog, magazine, or broadcast talk show may be appropriate for your circumstances; then again, maybe not. How do they know for sure what steps are appropriate for the unique path you are on? Additionally, it becomes very confusing when receiving conflicting advice from multiple sources. Broadcast and print media writers use emotionally charged adjectives like "soar" and "plunge" to describe the mostly routine daily ups and downs of the financial markets. These terms are specifically designed to invoke emotional impact. Would you ride an elevator that only provided "plunge" or "soar" button choices rather than "up" or "down?" I didn't think so. I'd take the stairs as well.

Money topics are emotional. The best advice when it comes to investment emotion is to remain in the middle between the two extremes of fear and greed. A little bit of each is OK. Too much and you may find yourself wishing you hadn't done what you did. Unfortunately, everyone has a book of regrets. The goal here is to limit new chapters from appearing in yours.

If your temperament is such that you have difficulty remaining calm when the media are frantically reporting the latest crisis du jour, consider changing the channel or turning the media source off.

> **_Procrastination Risk_**—The risk of not taking action. Delaying taking an appropriate action. "I'll do it later."

Possible Causes for Procrastination Risk
- Fear of the unknown
- Lack of a written plan of action
- Lack of prioritization of goals
- No third-party professional accountability, perhaps because of not "finishing your homework."

Possible Risk-Mitigation Strategy for Procrastination Risk
- Seize the moment. Today is the day. Act.
- Assign yourself small, manageable projects and/or break larger projects down into more manageable parts.
- Hire someone to hold you accountable for actions you need to take.
- Accept the fact: You can't go to recess until your preparation homework is finished.

GOOD TO KNOW

Not acting on important financial matters creates a cost much greater than what would have originally been paid. Enough said!

STEP TWO: RISK ASSESSMENT EXERCISE

Now that we have identified and defined each retirement income security killer (RISK) group and learned about the possible causes of core risks and the risk-mitigation strategies for each, the next step is to assess which core risks represent the highest potential risk for you currently.

RISKs are dynamic, not static. Thus, they are migratory in nature. This means that certain core risks have a higher probability of occurring over different periods of your life. They, like the seasons in nature, will change with the seasons of your life.

During full-time employment years, the types of risks that can severely affect your future financial well-being are different from those of someone in the retirement season of life. For example, during younger working years, loss-of-employment risk is closely correlated to "personal risk" from events such as premature death, disability, long-term illness, or layoff. If you have dependents who rely on your income for support, an interruption to work income due to a personal risk coming to fruition will affect the household finances immediately and your future retirement hopes directly. These personal-event risks can be identified and transferred to an insurance company, which will, for the cost of a premium, assume the risks of a specific event (providing an income replacement in the event of a loss) on your behalf. If a core personal risk should occur, the insurance company would pay the claim for the insured amount to the beneficiary. If the risk never occurred, the owner of the policy paid a cost for a risk transfer that didn't occur but enjoyed the peace of mind that if it had occurred, the insured had a plan to protect the estate and loved ones from potential peril.

Closer to your retirement, personal-event risks may diminish while other core risks such as asset allocation, sequence of return, uninsured medical expenses, and periodic financial-market fluctuation risks become more acute.

You do not need to be within view of your retirement to see the benefit from the exercise of identifying high-impact, core risks to your future-income plans. Mitigating core risks associated with retirement years early in your accumulation phase will improve your future retirement readiness. Also, early education about what hazards lie ahead will equip you with knowledge about avoiding potential future risks now versus later.

The closer you are to your expected retirement-recess launch, the more critical is a RISK assessment to improve your odds of remaining financially secure throughout your retirement-recess lifetime. In summary, you are never too young or too old to complete this homework. All ages benefit.

Homework:
Complete a RISK-profile assessment.

The goal of this homework step is to evaluate and identify financial, economic, and personal core risks that have a high probability of impacting your financial health if and when they do occur. A RISK-mitigation plan of action can then be developed to manage each risk appropriately, beginning with potential high-impact risks first. A RISK-assessment questionnaire is available to download for free at www.retirementrecess.com/retire-ready-resource-center.

Based on your responses, the RISK-assessment questionnaire is designed to provide a starting point to identify and mitigate areas of potential concern. It also serves as a great tool for determining the initial focus for the financial planning process. Because comprehensive financial planning for retirement covers many areas, putting increased focus on any high-potential threats to retirement income prioritizes your plan and will ensure these hot spots are not overlooked during the planning process. Also, your personal situation might involve additional areas that are not being addressed on the RISK-assessment questionnaire. If you have concerns, you are encouraged to seek professional guidance for a more complete RISK-impact assessment.

The following example graphically illustrates the results of a hypothetical RISK-profile assessment.

After completing the assessment exercise, the participant and adviser (if applicable) can focus on a plan of action to mitigate the high-impact core risks (identified in this example as asset allocation, liquidity, lifestyle, uninsured medical costs, and life happens risks). The other medium-and low-impact core risks should also be assessed and monitored as well.

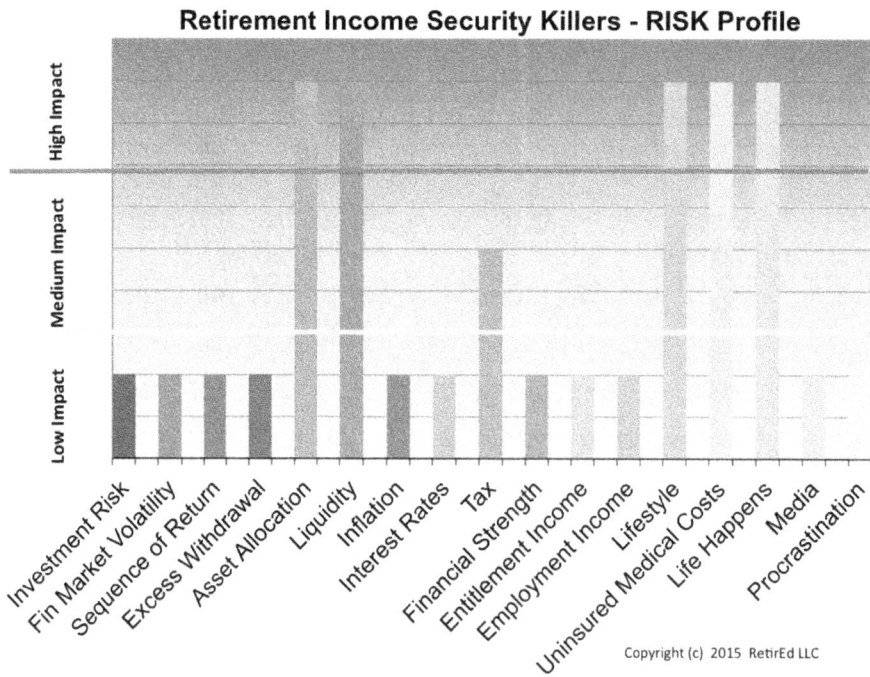

Retirement Income Security Killers - RISK Profile

Copyright (c) 2015 RetirEd LLC

STEP THREE: TAKING RISK MANAGEMENT MITIGATION ACTION OR—DO YOU FEEL LUCKY?

When it comes to risk showing up in our daily lives, some people seem to be luckier than others. Call it good karma or dumb luck; these "lucky ones" seem to skate through life mostly unharmed. Others, in the drama of their lives, go from one crisis to the next. Everyone who is now, or dreams of becoming, financially independent during the retirement years faces the same potential core risks. Some people are better equipped moneywise (referred to as capacity) than others to absorb the financial impact of an unexpected setback. Yet they and even the "lucky" are not exempt from the effects of each core risk we have identified. The fundamental question remains: Will you rely on continued luck alone to shape your retirement destiny or maybe allow procrastination to override necessary actions to shore up your retirement-income security? Or will you act decisively to manage the forces that can cut your retirement recess short? Your retirement destiny is awaiting your answer.

After completing the RISK-assessment homework exercise, a risk-mitigation management plan can be implemented. Many participants are shocked to discover that their risk-mitigation strategy thus far has been to assume high-impact risks by default. This is common for most folks until they learn that assuming risks by default, especially high-impact risks, can be a setup for early spend down of retirement assets or a roadblock for not reaching retirement on time if not corrected before the risk materializes in our lives. Of course, once you become aware that a core risk exists in your life, if you take no immediate action to mitigate it, you have exchanged assuming the risk for ignoring it. Let's agree that ignoring a potential high-impact risk does not change the fact that it still is there—unless you are in deep denial, in which case, it's still there, but you don't believe it is.

Core risks can be managed by one of the following four strategies: assume, ignore, avoid, or transfer. Let's take a look at each.

Assume

Unknowingly assuming the debilitating financial consequences of a retirement income security killer usually occurs by default when one doesn't know his or her retirement-income security is at risk. Once you are aware (after reading this book), steps can be taken to choose a strategy to avoid or transfer any high-impact core risks before they block the doorway to your retirement-recess adventure.

There are certain situations when "assuming" a risk becomes the chosen strategy: 1) You have accumulated sufficient wealth to financially self-fund or absorb a financial setback if and when it occurs. 2) You don't have sufficient funds to justify or afford the cost charged by a third party such as an insurance company to transfer the consequence of the potential risk from you to that third party. 3) You don't meet the qualifications of the transfer entity (insurance company) and have no means other than assuming the risk and hoping for a positive outcome. In this last instance, you are encouraged to consider additional strategies that might limit the damage caused by the assumption of a core risk. A competent financial adviser is equipped to help you in this area.

Ignore

Remember Alfred E. Newman's motto in *Mad* magazine? "What, me worry?" Pretending something that is there isn't there is not only delusional but also doesn't change the fact that the risk still exists. Those who consciously choose to ignore a risk usually do so because they don't want to emotionally deal with it, at least not at that moment. Take as an example the potential risk of dying without an estate plan of your making in place. As we discussed, death is not only a risk we all face every day; it's a 100 percent certainty to occur at some point. Even though no one is getting out of here alive, a huge percentage of people have no written will or estate plan for their survivors. Why is this? It isn't that they don't love their heirs; most people are simply uncomfortable thinking about and planning for the consequences of their own demise, so they ignore it and put it off. Or they are just too busy or they believe their meager net worth does not warrant completing this important assignment. Your documented wishes (in a will) are worth a fortune to your heirs regardless of your net worth if it keeps them from having to guess what you might have wanted them to do on your behalf.

Another reason a risk is ignored is the belief or hope that the risk won't become realized in your case. As mentioned, those who tend to be lucky enough in life to avoid many of the risks that plague others may be living with a false sense of security. Just when you think it won't happen to you—it does. You can be lucky in life and still have a once-in-a-lifetime event like a catastrophic uninsured medical expense and be financially wiped out faster than you can ask, "What, me worry?"

Avoid

Some risks are easier to avoid than others. To illustrate, if you believe the possibility of an in-flight disaster while flying on an airplane is too great a risk for your comfort level, you can choose to travel by other means and thus avoid the risk of flying. John Madden, the famous football coach and sports commentator, chose to travel in his custom road bus rather than fly on an airplane to each Monday Night Football game he cohosted. When you take action to avoid one risk, you often trade it for another. If you choose to take a bus rather than fly on an airplane, you avoid the risk of a plane crash, but you instead assume the risk of a possible traffic accident, which actually has a higher probability of occurrence than an air disaster.

Financially speaking, if you choose not to experience a permanent investment loss due to emotionally selling your investment at a loss during a periodic financial-market decline, you can avoid this risk by employing diversification and not liquidating the securities until their values recover—assuming they can and will recover. As you have read throughout this book, the ability to pause emotionally and allow financial markets and your investment account value to recover when their values are depressed is paramount in your future success.

Others choose to avoid the stock market and its associated potential risks completely. While not owning stocks in your retirement investment mix allows you to eliminate the risk associated with selling stocks at lower–than-purchased values during periodic market declines, you inadvertently may have increased other core risks such as inflation, interest rate, life happens, or excessive withdrawal—risks that threaten your financial well-being by other means.

If you already possess enough ready capital to fund your entire retirement lifestyle without any assistance from the inflation-fighting growth potential of the US stock market, why assume the risk when it is clearly not necessary? These financially fortunate ones can avoid the potential emotional swings associated with investment and financial-volatility risks because they have fully funded their retirement for life without the need for future capital appreciation. It's interesting to note that there are many wealthy people who have amassed enough money for a hundred lifetimes but still invest a portion of their fortunes in stocks. Reading their biographies often reveals why they choose to assume periodic financial-market volatility risk in hopes of something better. They see the price swings in the financial markets (volatility) as opportunity, not a detriment to their financial well-being.

If you are like most folks, and your retirement-planning analysis reveals a make-or-break necessity that at least part of your savings grows by the appreciation of common stock, seize the opportunity. Not owning stock (avoiding it) could be a greater risk to your financial well-being over time.

Transfer

Some potential risks to retirement-recess income are transferable to another entity. Insurance companies are in the risk-transfer business and are the primary commercial source of assuming your specified risk in exchange for a premium payment. Insurance policies for life, health, retirement income, disability income, long-term care, personal liability, home, and auto are all examples of risk-transference possibilities. Additionally, the risk of running out of income before the end of your life can also be transferred to an insurance company in the form of a series of guaranteed annuity payments.

Insurance companies calculate the odds of a risk occurrence plus the amount of liability involved and charge a premium to assume that risk. In simple terms, they are betting that the risk won't happen and the insured is betting it will. If you are right and a loss occurs, insurance companies have a contractual obligation to pay the claim. It's important to research the financial stability of the insurance company you are utilizing. Paying for a loss you incurred is contingent on the insurance company's ability to pay claims (financial strength-risk discussed earlier.) Think of an insurance company as a surrogate for a rich uncle—one who has told you that you can call if and when you have a financial loss and has promised to cover the cost for you. Don't have a rich and willing uncle to call? Then you can substitute an insurance company in his place—and pay a premium to have it on call if you should ever need it.

Homework:
Determine a high-potential RISK-mitigation plan
of actions as outlined above.

Download the worksheet at the end of the RISK-profile-assessment booklet at www.retirementrecess.com/retire-ready-resource-center.

STEP FOUR: MONITOR YOUR POTENTIAL RISK IMPACT REGULARLY

As we have discussed earlier, it's important to review potential RISK to your financial health on a regular basis (at least annually), as core risks can migrate in and out of your financial life over time. For example, when you and your spouse (if applicable) were in your younger earning years, you may have purchased life insurance to transfer the financial risk for those children depending on your income, which would cease if you died prematurely. In exchange for this transfer of risk from you to an insurance company, you paid a premium. As you survived each year and your children grew up and became financially independent of your support (yes, this does happen) and your net worth increased, your family's financial needs as beneficiaries decreased, and so did your need to transfer this risk to an insurance company. When reevaluating the need in this area, you may have discovered that the original reason to transfer the financial risk and the amount has changed. Many people wake up decades after purchasing life insurance to discover they have been paying premiums to transfer a risk that no longer exists or is greatly diminished. Ironically, when completing the risk-assessment exercise, you may discover you are overinsured for death and under-insured for conditions that don't kill you but decimate your retirement assets, such as uninsured long-term care costs. If this is true for you, a reallocation of premiums from life insurance policies to long-term care insurance may be needed.

Does your current retirement financial plan address all the pertinent core risks discussed earlier as the retirement income security killers, or RISK? Each core risk has the power, when left unmitigated, to threaten an early spend down of retirement assets either on its own or by triggering a chain reaction of other risks occurring.

Continue to use the RISK-assessment tool discussed earlier to evaluate the comprehensiveness and effectiveness of your existing or proposed retirement financial plan.

TAKE NOTE

YOUR RETIREMENT ASSETS ARE MOST VULNERABLE DURING THE TRANSITIONAL PERIOD (FIVE YEARS) PRECEDING AND FOLLOWING THE COMMENCEMENT OF YOUR RETIREMENT RECESS. YOUR CORE-RISK-MITIGATION HOMEWORK IDEALLY SHOULD BE FINISHED BEFORE YOU BEGIN YOUR RETIREMENT RECESS. IF YOU ARE ALREADY RETIRED, THE SOONER YOU BEGIN, THE BETTER.

RISK DOMINOES

RISK dominoes is not a game you want to play, especially during your retirement recess. One unmanaged core risk can trigger others, accelerating the spend down of retirement assets.

One example is making the mistake of underestimating the future cost of living (inflation risk) due to lack of knowledge and planning. For instance, take Flo, a retired administrator, who begins to live beyond her mostly fixed retirement-income source to fund her rising cost of living. This occurs because Flo failed to calculate the real costs of her future retirement lifestyle during her working years, while she had time to save and prepare for it. During her retirement, this underestimating of her true income needs caused an increase in lifestyle risk as she tried to maintain her rising standard of living without the benefit of a pay raise to support it. The tightening viselike effect of inflation squeezed Flo's living budget to the point where she felt she had less to live on each year. In effect, Flo's feelings were correct. As Flo redeemed more from her retirement account to compensate for her needs, she created an excessive-withdrawal risk that resulted in an earlier-than-planned, accelerated spend down of retirement investment assets. Her retirement asset spend down was further accelerated since distributions were coming from an investment that was overweighted in stocks (asset-allocation risk) that were in a temporary decline (periodic-financial-market-volatility risk), causing shares to be systematically redeemed at lower values than when they were originally purchased, creating a sequence-of-return risk. Finally, after spending down all assets, recess time was over, and the discouragement of becoming financially dependent on family and friends set in. It wasn't just a longer life span that caused the financial demise for Flo; it was failure to identify and mitigate early on the core risks of inflation and lifestyle long before the first domino fell.

Chapter Thirteen

Managing RISK Before and During Retirement Years

MANAGING RISK BEFORE RETIREMENT RECESS BEGINS

If you are years or decades away from ringing the retirement-recess bell, you may have discovered an important fact when you completed your RISK assessment. Most core risks with the greatest likelihood to threaten a financial setback during gainful employment years stem from personal events that include unemployment, disability, illness, death, and lawsuits. Fortunately, the financial consequences resulting from each of these events can be transferred to an insurance company prior to an occurrence in exchange for a premium payment. Other RISKs common to younger future retirees include asset allocation, liquidity, and inflation risks. The RISK assessment exercise is designed to help you identify such risks, evaluate the potential impact, and mitigate them before a financially damaging event occurs.

The one risk that causes more retirement failures than any other is also the one that is 100 percent within your control to manage: procrastination RISK. Time waits for no one, especially procrastinators.

Good intentions alone will not magically transport you to the playgrounds of the retirement recess you envision. The capital growth necessary to produce an increasing stream of income for a thirty- to forty-year retirement period requires three important ingredients: the money you invest both initially and on an ongoing basis; an investment return greater than the rising cost of living; and time to allow investment earnings to compound. Each year you wait to invest increases the amount of additional contributions and/or earnings necessary to reach the same financial goal. Remember Les the Procrastinator?

Most working folks have limited discretionary income beyond essential expenses to invest sufficiently for their futures. This makes contributing additional money from an already-stretched budget to make up for lost time nearly impossible to achieve. The consequence of falling behind due to procrastination often results in either attempting to earn higher investment returns (which increases periodic-financial-market-value-fluctuation risk) or delaying the retirement date and continuing to work (which increases employment risk) to accomplish the goal. The cost of waiting (procrastination risk) to fund your lifestyle plan will eventually increase to the point where you simply cannot accomplish it short of receiving an unexpected windfall like winning the lotto, for which odds are one in a kazillion. "So, you're telling me there is a chance!"

When asked, a large percentage or workers have no idea how much money they need to save from their paychecks to successfully fund their future lifestyle goals at their desired retirement age. Not knowing the amount of money that is required to accomplish your goal (lifestyle risk) on your terms is the equivalent of choosing to live your later years on someone else's terms (those of friends, family, or institutions).

Let's examine a hypothetical RISK profile assessment of Karen, a 40-year-old single professional who has a goal of retiring at age sixty five.

Retirement Income Security Killers - RISK Profile

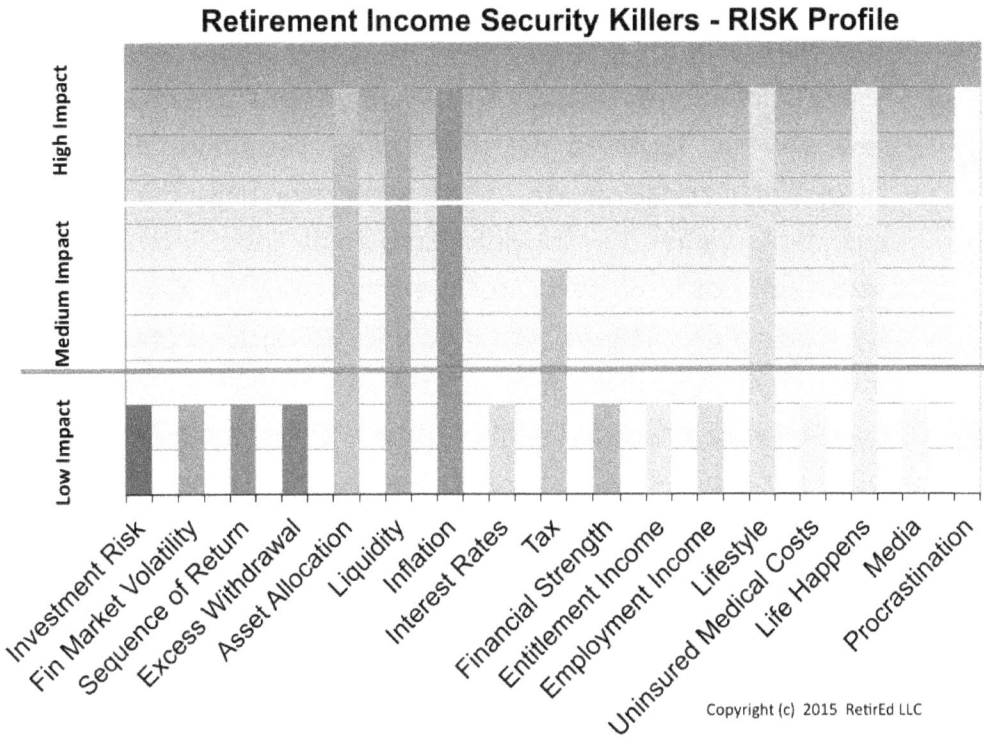

Copyright (c) 2015 RetirEd LLC

Notice that Karen's high-impact core risks include procrastination as well as other potential high-impact RISKs.

1. **Asset-Allocation Risk:** Karen's retirement account is invested primarily in an ultraconservative stable-value investment (100 percent money market). This is the case even though she has twenty-five years to work before she plans to draw income from this account to supplement her other retirement-income sources. The reason? The last financial market decline spooked her. The cause of this misalignment between her investment choice and

the long period of time she has before the money is needed is all too common. Due to the fear of yet another periodic financial market decline affecting her retirement account, Karen has chosen the certainty of retirement-account value (predictability) in the short-term. By doing so she has traded off the needed certainty of inflation-protected retirement income in her later years. She also has forfeited the tremendous compounding power of owning capital growth investments over long periods versus stable value—her low-interest-earning investments. Karen says she's not a risk-taker. Yet the great irony for Karen is that by choosing short-term certainty and failing to protect future investment income from inevitable and certain compounding cost-of-living increases (inflation), she is guaranteeing her future purchasing power will lose approximately 3 percent, or whatever inflation averages each year (minus the small amount she makes through her stable value account). Also, annual inflation increases do not stop when you stop working. Cost-of-living increases continue for as long as you do—a lifetime—and they always hit fixed-income retirees the hardest. By playing it safe in the short term, Karen, and millions like her, are losing future purchasing power when she and they most need it during retirement years. The result: If Karen persists in failing to realign her current investment strategy with her far-off retirement-income goals, she will either fall short of achieving her inflation-adjusted goal, or she will need to increase her contribution percentage amount significantly to accomplish the same money goal.

Karen can help mitigate the risk of underfunding her long-term retirement needs by changing her investment allocation. She can begin by reallocating her existing plan to produce long-term inflation protection and compounding capital growth. As a result, Karen will need to accept some periodic investment volatility in the short term for improved retirement-income protection in the long term. Additionally, it would be wise to add a calm-voice-of-reason professional financial adviser to manage both Karen's investment plan and her emotional swings during financial-market value gyrations. Adding this resource will help Karen remain focused on the long term by turning down the media noise during these often stressful but temporary emotional periods.

2. **Liquidity Risk:** By building a sufficient emergency cash reserve, Karen can forego the risk of robbing her retirement assets or being robbed by using high-interest credit cards as the only alternatives if and when a financial emergency (such as a new auto transmission) occurs. By systematically building up her cash reserves (in a savings account or money market account) to three to six months of essential expenses over time, Karen will possess a ready cash reserve to draw upon when needed. Karen also needs to build up liquid savings for fun goals like a vacation trip to Europe she dreams of and for the down payment on a new car she would like to drive one day. Completing a savings-priority exercise (an example is included in the homework workbook) will help Karen more efficiently prioritize her limited discretionary income across short-, mid-, and long-term savings objectives.

3. **Inflation Risk:** Karen can reduce this risk by resolving the investment-allocation risk discussed above.

4. **Lifestyle Risk:** Karen has not completed a detailed retirement-lifestyle exercise and determined how much money she will need to save during her working years to fund her chosen lifestyle as her retirement recess begins at age sixty-five. In doing

so, among other things, Karen will see the effects of her misaligned retirement investment account allocation discussed above. Karen is forty, and like all of us, will only be her current age for a year. Before she knows it, she will be wondering how time has passed so quickly. Now would be a great time for her to begin envisioning what she will *be-do-have* when her retirement-recess bell rings. Completing this homework as part of a comprehensive financial plan, Karen will become more emotionally invested in her later-life dreams rather than just investing blindly for a far-off future with no clear focus on what it all will mean.

5. **Life Happens Risk:** Karen has not written a will, power of attorney, or medical directive. After final expenses, her wishes are to leave her estate to her two minor age nephews in the event of her death. Karen was not aware that minor children couldn't inherit an estate directly. As a result, she will need to take estate-planning steps to ensure her nephews financially benefit as she wishes in the event of her death. Most estate-planning actions are relatively easy to complete during your lifetime, but not so much after the fact.

6. **Procrastination Risk:** Karen can avoid this infamous RISK by acting today. Like all of us, Karen will have one day less to accomplish her most important goals when tomorrow dawns.

Medium- and low-impact risks that are identified as the result of the RISK assessment exercise can be evaluated and addressed as well. The time invested in completing a RISK assessment as the starting point of the financial planning process might take forty-five to sixty minutes, tops. The resulting positive effects from avoiding a major financial setback as a result of this exercise could last a retirement lifetime.

MANAGING RISK DURING RETIREMENT YEARS

Once you cross over the bridge that separates the working-for-a-living group from the folks enjoying the retirement-recess playground, vulnerability to core risks increases. Why? It's simple. When you no longer earn income from full-time employment, the ability to recover from an unexpected risk event diminishes. In short, the inability to request a do-over for an unplanned, unexpected, and unmitigated negative financial event in retirement can accelerate the potential of a spend down of income resources.

The number of core risks from the list of seventeen directly affecting your wealth during retirement years can increase once your full-time-employment income ceases. It is important to complete an annual RISK-assessment exercise (discussed earlier) to identify high-impact core risks that may have migrated into your life since your last review and to decide on a mitigation strategy to manage each.

The following is a hypothetical RISK assessment for Ken, age seventy, who has been fully retired for three years. As you will learn, Ken has both limited financial assets and retirement income but does have substantial equity in his primary residence. Based on his responses to the RISK-assessment exercise and a review of his current financial picture, the following high-impact risks were identified for Ken:

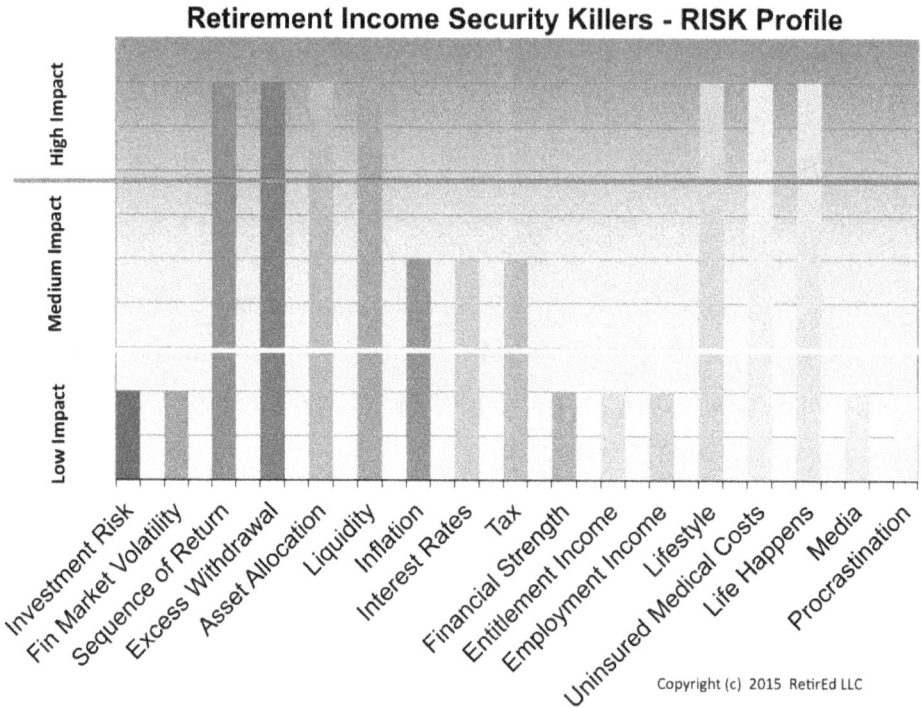

Retirement Income Security Killers - RISK Profile

Copyright (c) 2015 RetirEd LLC

1. **Sequence of Return:** Ken has established a systematic with-drawal amount from his IRA to supplement his income needs. His IRA is invested primarily in growth-stock mutual funds and because of systematic (monthly) distributions from this account, he could suffer permanent value loss if a periodic financial-market decline occurred concurrently. Because Ken is over age seventy and a half, annual required minimum distributions (RMD) from his IRA are mandated by the IRS. Ken will need to continue to withdraw RMD amounts each year to avoid a tax penalty of 50 percent on any required amount not withdrawn. His invest-ment account will need to be managed accordingly. Ken can address this core risk by choosing to reallocate some of his stock holdings to a cash (crash) reserve within his IRA to use dur-ing periodic financial-market declines.

2. **Excess Withdrawal:** Ken is presently withdrawing a monthly amount that exceeds a percentage of withdrawal that would assure Ken of not depleting his investment account too rapidly. Ken will need to consider reducing his current systematic withdrawal to equal the required minimum distribution amount mandated for IRA owners over the age of seventy and one half years. Ken will also need to review and consider eliminating some non-essential expenses to compensate for the lower monthly distribution from his IRA.

3. **Asset Allocation:** Ken's investable assets are currently overweighted (large percentage in one area) in small-company stock investments. Ken should rebalance his investment allocation to reduce his exposure to small-company stocks.

4. **Liquidity:** There is a lack of sufficient stable-value liquidity to provide income-supplement distributions during periodic financial-market declines (sequence-of-return risk) and for large emergency cash expenses. Ken could consider a reverse mortgage line of credit as a standby reserve strategy to cover these expenses as they occur.

5. **Lifestyle:** Ken is presently living beyond his investment-income capacity to supplement his rising cost of living. His current plan is dependent on a continued, uninterrupted rise in the stock market (unlikely) to fund his needs. In this situation, there are only two solutions: increasing income, which is limited when retired, or reducing expenses. It's easier to cut back some now rather than being forced to cut back a lot later.

6. **Uninsured Medical Expenses:** Ken does not have a contingency plan to fund uninsured medical expenses. He does not physically qualify for long-term, home-health-care insurance due to ongoing health issues. Home equity could be used to

cover medical costs through a reverse mortgage line of credit provided any illness does not require Ken to leave his home for an extended period. A prolonged absence from the home by the home/reverse mortgage owner beyond one year may force a foreclosure of the outstanding loan.

7. **Life Happens:** Ken does not have a valid power-of-attorney document or living trust to provide uninterrupted management for his financial affairs should he become incapacitated. Ken will need to review his estate-planning choices prior to becoming incapacitated.

Conclusion: Ken is not readily employable at this stage of his life. He also has a family history of longevity. To mitigate his high-impact core risks, Ken will need to make some tough decisions about eliminating nonessential expenses (wants and wishes) and consider downsizing his primary residence to make his financial ends meet for what could be an additional twenty to thirty years of retirement.

Completing retirement-readiness homework before and not after the recess bell rings affords more opportunity to fully fund a desired lifestyle without being told that recess time is over before you are finished playing.

To sum up, a RISK assessment can be completed at the onset of the formal financial planning activity to ensure the planning process addresses any core risks identified in the assessment. Many financial advisers use the RISK-assessment exercise as an effective tool to provide initial financial education on the importance of comprehensive retirement planning.

Think of the RISK-assessment exercise as both a prefinancial planning risk identifier and an annual checkup to identify any new concerns.

MIDTERM REVIEW

Thus far, we have covered several aspects of the financial and emotional preparations required to fund and protect a retirement-recess period. Regardless of your current age or retirement status, you may be feeling confident, overwhelmed, or somewhere in the middle. If you are part of the group feeling behind the ball, or even totally discouraged that the dream of financial independence has slipped beyond your reach, remember that absolute failure only occurs when you give up. You have the power to begin the financial planning process anytime you choose—even today. Especially today.

During your reading you may be discovering that the scope of financial planning necessary to thoroughly address all the aspects of preparing for a multi-decade retirement recess won't fit on an index card or a napkin—as a few financial authors would have you believe. What will fit on an index card are the key review points covered below.

- The sooner you engage in the strategic process of comprehensive financial planning, the greater your odds of success. You can only fail by never beginning.
- Comprehensive financial planning includes both the art of defining your desired retirement-life vision and the science of financial calculations, assumptions, and projections to determine your chosen lifestyle's ongoing funding requirements.
- Financial planning for retirement involves more than investment management. You could own the perfect investment (if it existed) and still run out of money in retirement if you failed to manage the risks that can create an earlier-than-expected spend down of money. There are seventeen retirement income security killers (RISK). Consider them all.
- There are more people who believe they can be their own retirement financial adviser than those who actually are equipped with the education, experience, and discipline to successfully do so.

It's helpful to keep in mind that you don't have to face the immensity of planning for your retirement alone. Imagine starting your primary education at age five and being told, "The goal is to successfully study and master all the learning objectives required to graduate from high school twelve years from now. Here are some books and internet sites to help you. And by the way, make sure you allow yourself to be influenced by outside sources who don't know you personally (broadcast and print media) and who offer conflicting information about your education." Without the support, encouragement, and special skills of parents, teachers, aids, counselors, and coaches we happen to meet along the way, I doubt anyone would graduate—let alone be equipped to face adult life successfully.

The same can be said for getting your retirement-preparation homework finished. Compared with preparing for primary careers, no one spends a fraction of that time planning for retirement. Yet retirement could last longer than all the years you worked for a living. For a growing number of folks, competent financial professionals (personal tutors) are needed to help with the essential lessons and required financial homework assignments to ensure your successful graduation from a working career to retirement recess.

Home-schooled (do-it-yourself) retirement planning is appropriate for a select group of people. If you are not sure if you qualify as a self-directed (DIY) retirement-planning candidate, the next chapter was written to help you decide. I have included objective (nonbiased) information about how to locate, vet, interview, and hire a retirement-planning professional—one who will guide you from the financial classroom to the retirement-recess playground before you are too old to enjoy it. Spoiler alert: It is not me. Remember my promise about no infomercial?

Chapter Fourteen

Hiring a Lifetime Financial Adviser

Everyone arrives at a time in life when he or she must decide who, if anyone, will assist with the critically important work of transforming retirement lifestyle dreams and goals into reality. What initially begins in early working years as a relatively simple self-directed financial plan consisting mostly of investment accounts and insurance programs grows more complex as life moves forward and variables multiply. Most people simply outgrow the capacity to manage their own financial affairs long before they realize it. The time to make the transition from a "do it myself" plan to an "I need professional help with my planning" strategy is before, and not after, you make an expensive financial mistake.

It's not always easy to ask for help. After all, most of us have been raised to be self-sufficient and independent. Asking for help can sometimes feel like failure when, in reality, knowing you need assistance in a particular facet of your planning and seeking it is a step toward securing absolute success—a sign of financial maturity that can occur at any age.

HOW'S YOUR T?

How do you know when you need professional financial assistance? One way to determine whether you should seek a professional financial guide at this stage of your planning is to take the "How's Your T?" test. (No, I'm not referring to the hormone testosterone.)

Ask yourself whether you possess enough of the three Ts—time, training, and temperament—to successfully prepare for, implement, monitor, and protect the lifestyle goals of a financial plan that will ultimately decide the quality and degree of independence you are hoping to enjoy.

Specifically, do you have sufficient *time* to dedicate not only to the initial financial planning activities but also time for the continual updates that will need attention for your entire retirement-recess period? Retirement planning is an ongoing process spanning both the before- and during-retirement years. The retirement financial plan does not retire when you do. In fact, once you make the transition from the phase of asset accumulation (working years) to income distribution (retirement decades), your financial plan requires increased time management to ensure income continues to flow uninterrupted each and every month.

Do you have the *training* to understand the technical terms and planning strategies that will need to be evaluated, chosen, and implemented? Also, as things change—in the world, the economy, and with you—whom will you rely on for your continuing education? Is a third-party resource such as a blogger, newsletter writer, or on-the-air financial advice giver really providing you unbiased, independent facts and information, or is there a potential conflict of interest because that person ultimately guides you to purchase a specific product or service that benefits that person first and you second? How will you really know for sure what the real motives are?

Last, and perhaps most important of all, do you have the *temperament* or emotional discipline to stick with the plan even when financial times get tough? Do you have the confidence and personality to be your own *calm voice of reason* during periods of crisis and uncertainty?

When thinking about each of the three Ts we just discussed, how would you rate yourself in each area? Consider both your current capabilities and what they might be ten to twenty years from now.

Homework:

Do a self-assessment of your abilities to be your own financial adviser: strong, average, or weak.

Three Ts	In the Past	Currently	10 years from now	20 years from now
Time (Focus)				
Training (Education)				
Temperament (Discipline)				

A caution about conducting self-appraisals of your abilities: Studies show that as many as seven of ten people believe they are fully capable (a rating of "strong" for the three Ts) of being their own financial planner. Yet upon closer examination, only two in ten have sufficient time, training, and temperament to fully qualify.

If you rated yourself average or weak in any of the three T categories, your next assignment is to locate a lifetime financial adviser who
scores "strong" in each T area.

FINANCIAL ADVISER—TEACHER, TUTOR, ADVOCATE

The ultimate retirement goal for most folks is to graduate from the
work-for-a-living classroom to the lavish playgrounds of their retirement recess with enough financial resources and time to fully enjoy the
fruits of long labors with as little worry as possible. To do so successfully requires mastering specific learning objectives as well as completing preparation assignments and homework, much of which I am
outlining in this book.

No learning environment is complete without a qualified instruc-
tor who thoroughly understands the subject material. For those who
have decided not to put their most important years at risk by going it
alone, investing the time to locate, investigate (vet), interview, and hire
a qualified financial adviser may be one of the best investments ever.

LIFETIME FINANCIAL ADVISER (LFA)

The title lifetime financial adviser (LFA) is not an officially recognized
title or designation within the financial services industry. It is a label
I created for this book, used to describe recommended attributes of
the ideal professional or firm (legal entity) to assist you in completing
all your financial and emotional homework. An LFA is a firm or person
who will faithfully help you fully prepare for and keep you centered on
the winding path of your retirement journey. Anyone who subsequently
adopts this title is doing so without my expressed confirmation that the

person meets or exceeds the seven Cs ideals discussed in this chapter.

There are two primary focuses for retirement-planning services. One is the traditional money-management side and the other is retirement-lifestyle planning. Many financial advisers concentrate on the science—or financial advice and money-management aspects—of retirement planning. They are most interested in helping their clients manage their investment assets and use retirement-planning software programs to create cash flow assessments to determine the probability of how long money will last based on a variety of assumptions.

A smaller but growing group of financial advisers focus on the lifestyle-planning aspects of retirement. They assist their financial planning clients in defining specifically what their retirement will look like throughout their retirement lifetime. As life expectancy continues to increase, a growing number of preretired people are interested in developing a retirement-life plan tailored to what they want to be *(relevance)* and *do (living purposely)* in addition to what they hope to *have (experience)*. Locating and engaging a financial adviser who is balanced in providing both the science (financial math) and art (life-plan development) of financial planning expertise is ideal.

A LIFETIME FINANCIAL ADVISER (LFA) DESCRIPTION

An LFA listens carefully as you describe your lifestyle vision goals, and provides a comprehensive financial plan to help you obtain and protect those goals. In other words, he or she offers a balanced financial planning approach incorporating both the art of retirement lifestyle planning and the science of funding and protecting it from the perils of an early spend down. An LFA tutors you in areas that require extra attention, assigns preparation homework, holds you accountable for completing it on time, and introduces you to other professionals who can assist you in areas that require specialized attention. Most importantly, an LFA teaches you rather than tells you what to do.

LOCATING A POTENTIAL LFA

A good matchmaker resource is often someone you already know and trust. Start with the reliable professionals who know you personally. CPAs, income tax preparers, and attorneys who know you through a current professional relationship may also be aware of a retirement-planning professional who fits the description of an LFA who could be a perfect match for you. Additionally, ask work associates, friends, and family members whom they trust for retirement-planning guidance. Finally, there are several professional financial planning associations that refer their members and the public to potential LFA candidates. They are the following:

- *The Financial Planning Association® (FPA®)* (http://www. plannersearch.org/). The FPA® is the largest membership organization for CERTIFIED FINANCIAL PLANNERS™ (CFP® professionals) in the US, and it includes members who support the financial planning process.
- *The National Association of Personal Financial Advisers (NAPFA)* (http://www.napfa.org/). The NAPFA is the country's leading professional association of fee-only financial advisers.
- **Find a CFP® professional** (www.cfp.net). Although many professionals call themselves "financial planners," only CERTIFIED FINANCIAL PLANNERS™ have completed extensive training and are held to the highest ethical and educational standards.

PROFESSIONAL TITLES AND DESIGNATIONS

Typical industry professional titles include wealth manager, financial adviser, investment adviser, and financial planner. It's important to know that currently there is no academic, educational, or experiential requirement for a person to use one of the above titles.

In addition to a professional title, many advisers possess professional designations that require successfully passing exams and possessing a certain level of work experience and continuing education to maintain the designation. Examples include the following: CERTIFED FINANCIAL PLANNER™ (CFP®), Chartered Life Underwriter (CLU), Chartered Financial Consultant (ChFC), Chartered Financial Analyst (CFA), and Chartered Retirement Planning Counselor (CRPC®). Using these professional designations requires that the holder complete specific ongoing academic requirements and remain in good standing within the financial services industry and the public.

Professional credentials are important indicators of credibility and commitment, but they don't necessarily guarantee the holder will provide you with comprehensive retirement-planning services in actual practice. Some credentialed professionals choose to focus on a single aspect of retirement planning such as investments, estate, or insurance planning in actual practice.

No matter how large or small your current net worth or age, your goal is to seek, find, and employ someone who offers *comprehensive* (both science and art) retirement financial planning services.

VETTING THE FINANCIAL ADVISER

Homework:
Conduct a preinterview background check.

Taking the time to conduct a preinterview background check prior to your initial interview appointment can save valuable time in the event your investigation turns up negative or incomplete information. Here are a few suggestions of resources to check prior to your first interview appointment:

- **Third-Party Professional Referral Sources**. If the potential LFA was referred to you by a professional third party such as your CPA or attorney, ask the third party about the strong points of this professional or firm and why the third party feels he or she would be a good fit for you. Also ask what the feedback response has been with others who were referred by this entity. It's also appropriate to ask the referring source if there is any business connection between the source and the potential LFA. Although paid referral agreements are rare, they pose a potential conflict of interest and should be evaluated carefully.

- **Adviser Website**. Search and access the potential LFA's website on the internet. If there isn't one, note this in the "communications" section of the evaluation worksheet, and when you meet with the prospective LFA, inquire why he or she chose not to provide this valuable communications tool to clients and the public at large. If the LFA maintains a website, does it convey a message that feels comfortable to you? Click on the services offered section. Do the services referenced describe a comprehensive retirement planning process or only information specific to a single area such as investments or insurance? Does the website describe an adviser who is holistic and financial plan-centric or investment-centric in nature? You are searching to find an authentic plan-centric adviser, not an investment-centric entity disguising itself as focused on financial planning. Also, is the site current or are you finding outdated (more than six months old) materials posted on it?

- **Internet Search**. Do an individual name search for the prospective LFA on an internet search engine. If there is no information, this is not necessarily a negative. But information that contains a complaint and/or litigation is a flashing stop sign to drop this LFA candidate from your search list.
- **Background Check**. Conduct a search by individual and business name by accessing these primary sites:
  - **Financial Industry Regulatory Authority (FINRA) at** http://brokercheck.finra.org. (The link is now a requirement on all broker/adviser websites.) This site will allow you to view information about both registered representatives and broker/dealer firms associated with FINRA.
  - **Investment Adviser Public Disclosure website** at http://www.adviserinfo.sec.gov/. This site provides information about registered investment advisers (RIAs) and firms registered as RIA companies.
- **Other background resources include the following:**
  - Verification of an individual's CFP® certification and background at BrightScope (360-Degree Financial Adviser View) at http://www.BrightScope.com.
  - State-specific insurance license verification – search by specific state

- Professional designation current-status check – search by specific designation

If everything checks out to your satisfaction during the preinterview background investigation, the next step is to schedule a one-hour introductory appointment with the LFA.

Optional: Preinterview—Seven Cs Financial Adviser Profile— Question and Answer Worksheet

Prior to scheduling your face-to-face introductory appointment, download and send the Seven Cs Financial Adviser Profile Q&A form prior to your appointment date. The worksheet can be downloaded from the Extra Credit section at www.retirementrecess.com/retire-ready-resource-center. When forwarded to the adviser along with your request that it be completed, this form allows the potential LFA to answer all questions and requests for information that are covered during the Seven Cs Financial Adviser Assessment exercise prior to the introductory appointment.

REQUESTING AN INITIAL INTERVIEW

Notice how responsive and professional the adviser is to your request for an informational interview. What preinterview information, if any, did the LFA make available to you to assist with the interview process? If sent, was the Seven Cs Financial Adviser Assessment Q&A form completed prior to your appointment?

When you entered the LFA office, what kind of greeting did you receive? Did the atmosphere feel calm and organized, or was it loud and frantic?

Was the office in good order? Piles of files lying on desks and counters speak loudly about the overall organization of the LFA and current workload. That could be your financial life in a file on the bottom of a large paper pile.

On your exit from the interview meeting, ask for a quick tour of the entire office. This is an unusual request, but it should be honored if you ask. Observe the scene behind the proverbial curtain. Everyone has a visitor-friendly lobby or conference room, but what does the back office look like? That's the place where your plan and investment accounts are actually serviced.

THE SEVEN Cs FINANCIAL ADVISER ASSESSMENT

A diamond is graded by evaluating four quality characteristics referred to as the Four Cs: cut, clarity, color, and carat. When determining the quality characteristics of a potential LFA, use the following seven Cs: character, commitment, communication, competence, connections, comprehensiveness, and compensation. A seven Cs evaluation worksheet is provided at the end of this section for your use.

> **Character:** The mental and moral qualities distinctive to an individual.

- **Personality.** Consider first the adviser's temperament. As with all professions, there are a wide variety of personalities to choose from. *Does his or her personality feel harmonious with yours?* Type A—active, energetic, driven. Type B—laid back, methodical. Type ZZZZ—boring, serves as a sleep aid.
- **Compatibility.** Pay attention to your comfort level during the initial interview. *Do you feel comfortable,* or *do you feel*

uneasy? The process of financial planning may be a bit intimidating, especially if this activity is new for you. It is very important that the person chosen to take you forward through what at times can feel like an overwhelming process has the ability to put you at ease. The adviser should feel like your advocate and not an adversary. In essence, you should feel cared for in a holistic way. *Do you sense you are heard and that your feelings and circumstances are understood?*

The art and science of comprehensive financial planning for retirement requires that difficult choices sometimes need to be made in a timely manner. However, you should never feel pressured to take action before you are emotionally ready. This includes the decision to engage the adviser to work with you.

- **Conflicts of interest.** *Does the potential adviser put your financial interests first?* A potential conflict occurs when circumstances within the adviser's personal and/or professional life bring into question the possibility of other interests being sought before yours. An example could be the adviser having a special compensation arrangement with an investment or insurance program sponsor. Although these arrangements have become rare over the past few years, the question arises: Is the program being recommended because it meets your needs or because of a bonus paid to the adviser if you purchase a product or program?

  Not all potential conflicts of interest are compensation based. An example of a noncompensation potential conflict of interest has to do with the amount of time the adviser spends on activities outside the realm of personal financial planning. Too much time devoted to outside interests could impede the adviser's ability to properly supervise your financial planning objectives. Is he or she spending more time on the book tour or speaking at conferences than tending to your financial planning interests? The potential adviser's website might give you clues about outside interests such as speaking events, editorializing, and book tours. Ask the following: *Are there any potential or real conflicts of interest between the outside and inside activities of the adviser and that adviser's primary responsibilities for my financial well-being?* If so, *where are they fully disclosed for my review prior to engagement?*

Financial advisers who are registered investment advisers or representatives of a registered investment adviser firm must disclose any conflicts of interest in writing within the company business brochure, often referred to as ADV Part II, which is required to be given to you before you engage the LFA.

Fiduciary Standard

A "fiduciary" is a person or firm that adheres to the highest standard of putting customers' interests before their own in all their activities by operating in a way that is ethical, transparent, and beyond reproach.

Some financial advisers provide a written fiduciary pledge to their existing and prospective clients. Stating in writing or orally that one adheres to a strict standard as a "fiduciary" is fine, but remember, actions speak louder than words. The Seven Cs Financial Adviser Assessment is designed to help you identify financial advisers who naturally practice their profession with only the highest ethical standards regardless of governmental attempts to regulate a minimum fiduciary standard of conduct on all financial advisers. The financial professionals who consistently rate high in all seven C areas of this assessment are most likely to not only say the right things but also focus on a high stand of fiduciary care in what they *do* for you.

> **Commitment:** *The state or quality of being dedicated to a cause or activity.*

- **Dedication.** Ask the following: *What professional designations have you earned? Have you earned any professional or industry recognitions?* Be aware that just because a firm may manage a large amount of investment assets, this fact by itself is not the only measurement of professional commitment. In addition to professional designations and recognitions, assess how committed the prospective LFA is in helping you achieve your lifetime retirement goals. Remember, promises kept are more important than promises made. Ask the following: *What is your greatest challenge in helping your clients achieve their goals? How do you assist your clients in overcoming these obstacles of success?*

- **Accountability.** Commitment only works if each party honors the respective commitments to the relationship. A fully committed LFA will hold you accountable for completing homework assignments on a timeline you both agree to honor.
  Ask the following: *How will you ensure that I keep my commitments to you and myself toward achieving my goals? What specific process will be followed to make sure homework assignments are completed on time? How can you assure me that you will remain as committed to my goals as I am?*

- **Ongoing client-education programs.** A hallmark of a fully committed LFA is ongoing client-education programs. That's not merely infomercials about investing more money or referring others to them, but true noncommercial education programs, including timely retirement topics outside the realm of the LFA's practice. Topics like maintaining physical and emotional health in retirement and good nutrition habits are popular subjects. Ask the following: *What continuing education programs do you make available to your client families? How are continuing education programs delivered—via classroom, the internet, or newsletter?*

Communication: *The act or process of using words, sounds, signs, or behaviors to express or exchange information or to express your ideas, thoughts, and feelings to someone else.*

Notice during the initial information meeting whether the communication between you and the potential LFA is balanced or one-sided. *Who's doing the talking and listening?* Is the potential LFA talking at seventy-five words a minute with gusts to two hundred, or is the LFA's communication cadence slower, with pauses, to check for your understanding? In addition to evaluating the balance and clarity of communication demonstrated by the potential LFA during your initial conversations, *request specific examples of written and electronic communications that clients receive, and ask about the frequency with which they are sent or made available to you.*

- **Clarity.** *Ask the LFA candidate to explain in his or her own words the retirement planning **process** used with clients similar to you.* Is it clear, comprehensive and, most importantly, understandable to you? Does it fully address what you believe to be your most important planning needs, or is it a generic "one size fits all"? *Will the completed financial plan be delivered as a printed copy, electronic file, or both? If electronic, what capabilities are available for you to remotely review your plan?*
- **Progress reports.** *Inquire about when you will receive investment*

program statements and other financial planning communications and how—electronic, mail, or both. Are investment statements and transaction summaries sent directly from a third-party custodian or from the financial adviser's office?

Note: For financial security purposes, always request that investment account statements be sent from a third-party account custodian rather than from the adviser's office directly. This way you know your investment statements accurately account for your money as reported from each primary source without any risk of manipulation by the LFA.

- **Investment discretion.** *Does the financial adviser make changes to your investment portfolio (buy-sell) without your permission, which is referred to as "investment discretion," or are all transactions preapproved by you prior to action? Do you have a choice in this matter?*

- **Cost disclosure**. *How are costs for services communicated? Is there full transparency of all costs prior to engagement? You should leave the interview meeting with a good understanding of approximate costs for services if you end up hiring this potential LFA.*

- **Personal identification information protection.** Inquire as to what personal information and account security measures are used to safeguard your personal information from identity theft, fraud, and security breaches. Ask the following: *Has there been a breach of security in the past for this LFA? If so, what was the result of the investigation, and what steps have been taken to deter further breaches of personal information?*

- **Requests for service and information.** *Ask whom you will be communicating with when you call in to ask a question or to make a request. Is it the adviser, the assistant, or someone else?*

- **Out-of-state services.** Many advisers have the ability to e-communicate remotely to clients living out of the immediate service area. If you reside out of state or are temporarily out of the home state of the adviser, or if you move out of state in the future, *is the adviser properly licensed in that region and is it possible to maintain the relationship remotely? If not, does the potential LFA have a professional out-of-state network of fellow LFAs for an introduction if you relocate?*
- **Communication methods.** *What communication methods are used to stay in touch with you?* The most common choices are email, texting, telephone, in-person meetings, and regular mail. *Were you asked what communication method you preferred?*

Competence: *Possession of required skills, knowledge, and qualification.*

When you think about competence, think surgeon. Let's say you're scheduling a tricky surgery and you have a preop meeting with the surgeon who will be on the other end of the knife. You want to hear about successful experiences with this procedure—which is new to you but not to him or her. Each step of the upcoming operation is explained to you in plain English without hesitation, eye to eye. Look for the same signs of competence with a potential LFA—the adviser should be educated, relaxed, organized, experienced, and confident.

- **Education and experience.** Your preinterview research homework should have produced a clear picture of education and experience. If not, ask about both in the interview. Years of experience don't necessarily make a person right, but long experience does provide a sense of competence that no other attribute can.

Ask the potential LFA why he or she chose to do this important work. Why this profession? Listen for personal stories rather than generic responses. Here's an example: "I started in this business a long time ago to make a living and help people. Somewhere along the way the order reversed—I found myself helping people as a living. It's the most honorable job I could ever think of performing." Ask the following: *How long do you intend to do what you do? If you leave, whom will I be working with going forward? Does this LFA have a succession plan? If yes, what is it? If no, why not?*

- **Specialist or Generalist.** *Is this professional a specialist in retirement planning or a generalist trying to look like a specialist?* A generalist knows a little bit about many topics. A specialist knows a lot about a limited number of topics. *If LFAs state that they specialize, ask for specifics as to why they consider themselves specialists. Ask for examples of profiles of the client families they currently serve. Are they similar to your profile or more eclectic in nature?*

> **Connections:** *Relationships in which persons, things, or ideas are linked or associated with something or someone else.*

A well-established LFA has a network of professional service resources to help assist in addressing retirement-planning issues that fall outside the scope of the LFA's specialized practice. Examples include an estate attorney for drafting a will, a power of attorney, a living will, and a trust (if applicable); a tax preparer to answer tax questions and file income tax returns, if needed; a health-insurance professional to assist with securing health insurance and Medicare supplement policies; and a real estate and mortgage professional for real estate matters.

A professionally connected LFA is able to facilitate referral services for you with other professionals who, with your written permission, can collaborate together and bring their areas of expertise to the planning table for your benefit.

If you already have established professional relationships with a tax preparer and estate attorney, ask if the LFA will supply third-party release requests giving your permission for any or all professionals who service your needs a chance to collaborate on your behalf.

Another important connection is between the financial adviser and the adviser's succession plan. Simply stated, the question is this: *Who will run the business if the financial adviser is unable to perform duties due to disability or death?* All financial advisers should have a current succession plan that will, among other things, immediately connect you to available professionals who will continue to provide for your needs. Many financial advisers do not have any such plan in place.

Two other succession questions are these: *When are you planning on leaving the business? Are there any plans to merge your practice in the near term with another financial planning entity?*

Comprehensiveness: *Completeness over a broad scope; inclusive.*

How extensive are the retirement planning services offered by the potential LFA? Is the primary focus on one aspect of retirement planning, such as investments or insurance, or do services extend over all nine core areas listed below? Is there a written financial plan for you to follow? If so, does it include recommendations for mitigating the core risks to your retirement income we discussed earlier? Request a sample copy of a typical retirement financial plan.

As previously mentioned, many financial advisers who promote themselves as "retirement-planning professionals" are focused on a single component or two of retirement planning. A high score for comprehensiveness and fiduciary responsibility can only be earned by the LFA who focuses attention on each of the following areas of retirement financial planning:

- Retirement life planning goals (What you want to *be-do-have*).
- A statement of current net worth.
- A report of essential and nonessential expenses.
- A statement of retirement planning assumptions.
- A report of retirement cash flow by year from retirement age to end of life expectancy.
- An investment plan, including a personalized written investment policy and an outline of the plan's management.
- Insurance planning (all areas, not limited to life and/or long-term care insurance).
- Tax planning, including an investment distribution prioritization exercise.
- Estate planning, including a will, power of attorney, medical directive, trust, and beneficiary review.

Ask the following: *If I engage you or your firm, how will you help me identify which core risks have the highest potential to negatively affect my financial health, and how will you assist me in mitigating them now and in the future?*

Also ask these questions: *What is the name of the software program you use to produce financial plans for your clients? Why do you or your firm use this particular program? Will it be available to me online, or do I contact you for updates?* If the adviser points to his or her yellow pad and calculator when asked this question about software, politely conclude the meeting and leave.

> **Compensation:** *The tender exchanged for a product or service.*

Great LFAs are not too good to be true, but they are too good to be free. If you lack the three Ts (time, training, and temperament) to manage your own retirement planning details for the rest of your lifetime and to manage the provision of a legacy for the next generation, the value you receive from your calm-voice-of-reason LFA can make the compensation paid to the LFA well worth it. In other words, if the skill and wisdom of your LFA can help you avoid a foolish, unguided financial mistake that could result in an early spend down of your retirement assets, the amount you pay the LFA could be returned to you many times in added value.

Numerous articles have been written that treat financial adviser fees as 100 percent cost with no intrinsic benefit. Recent studies conclude that a professional financial adviser can add as much as 2–5 percent annually to your investment value through his or her guidance. What is your ultimate success really worth? The undisclosed potential cost created by the "free" retirement-planning blogger who, without knowing your financial planning abilities, is promoting the idea that you can be your own LFA, is simply too high for most people to afford.

There are different methods for compensating a financial adviser: commission, fee based, fee only, flat fee, hourly, salary, retainer, and beads for bucks (just kidding). Within the financial services industry and media there is an ongoing debate over which compensation method is best suited for the consumer in terms of providing objective advice and reducing potential conflicts of interest. An open discussion about the advantages and disadvantages of different compensation methods is healthy for this and any industry, right up to the point where the debate becomes self-serving and accusatory. Unfortunately, there seems to be an increase of accusations about compensation structures where contempt precedes investigation.

If you interview several professionals whose practices represent a different compensation method from their peers, you will most likely find each at some point defending his or her chosen compensation structure while defaming the character of those who choose to be compensated differently. Character defamation based solely on how someone chooses to be compensated without evidence of actual conflicts of interest or questionable business practices presents you with an opportunity to reconsider the character assessment of the accuser.

As with any industry, all compensation methods within the financial services realm have advantages and disadvantages. As a consumer of financial products and services, it is your responsibility to understand what compensation choices are available and which method you are most comfortable in using. Bottom line: One compensation structure versus another by itself does not necessarily determine the level of service you will ultimately receive or whether the adviser will act in your best interest. In the end, the in-your-best-interest question is more a matter of character than compensation.

The following is a brief description of the most basic compensation methods and some advantages and disadvantages of each:

Commission—This was the primary method of compensation when the financial services industry was in its infancy. In this method, the client pays an amount that is usually a percentage of the investment in a specific product or service. In the case of mutual funds, it can be charged up-front (sales load), upon liquidation (surrender charge) and/or as an ongoing annual fee (under section 12b-1 of the Investment Company Act of 1940). Active mutual funds also have internal management fees that are part of the overhead of running the mutual fund. Mutual fund management fees vary and do not compensate the adviser recommending the fund. Tax-deferred variable annuities usually have no up-front charge, but they do have an ongoing annual mortality and expense (M&E) charge, and they may or may not have a surrender charge upon liquidation. The investment funds used within a tax-deferred variable annuity have separate management fees. Mutual funds and variable annuities are sold by prospectus, which is a legal document outlining all fees and costs to the investor. Insurance products such as life, disability, and long-term care policies typically build a commission into the premium that compensates the issuing insurance agent.

Pros: Commission-based financial advisers may offer other financial services—such as financial planning—at no additional cost to their clients. Mutual fund commissions are charged one time when money is initially invested, with no reoccurring up-front costs on invested money. Capital gains and dividends are reinvested with no up-front sales charge. Lower commission costs may be obtained through multiple investments within the same investment mutual fund family; they're called "rights of accumulation." Additionally, larger investments into a family of mutual funds are purchased with lower initial sales charges, called "break points." As with other commissionable products such as mortgage loans, investment and insurance commission costs can vary from one company to another.

Cons: The label "commission" has a negative connotation that implies dishonesty. Some, but certainly not all, commission-based financial advisers focus on making a product sale first rather than offering a balance of sales, service, and advice. In the past, some commission products incentivized the adviser by offering bonuses based on total sales of a financial product. In recent years, there has been a sharp decline in the offering of sales-incentive programs. Most commission bonus programs have been eliminated due to potential conflicts of interest. Because commission costs are embedded into the transaction and not paid as a separate amount, costs are not readily transparent. An investment product prospectus discloses all costs but can be difficult for the average investor to fully understand before investing money.

Fee-Only Compensation—This compensation method is offered by advisers who desire no affiliation with commission-based products or services companies. They work on a fully disclosed fee for services such as hourly, flat, retainer, subscription, and percent of assets managed.

Pros: The adviser only offers programs and services that charge a percentage fee for management or an hourly or flat amount. There is no implied or actual conflict of interest due to commission compensation.

Cons: If a client's financial plan requires purchasing products that traditionally charge a commission, such as life insurance, disability income insurance, or long-term care insurance, the client most likely will need to seek commission-based products outside the main scope of the adviser's practice in order to purchase the needed investment or insurance product.

Fee-Based Compensation—This is a combination of fee and commission models previously described. The typical adviser charges an hourly or flat-fee rate for financial planning services, a percentage cost to actively manage noncommission investment plans, or chooses to include financial planning services within an asset management fee model. Also, the adviser may recommend, manage, and directly service programs that typically pay a commission such as load mutual funds; immediate, fixed, and variable annuities; and life, disability income, and long-term care insurance.

Pros: Offering a comprehensive assortment of products and services that include both commission and fee-based programs allows clients to receive comprehensive management and servicing from a single source.

Cons: This compensation method is sometimes misunderstood by the client to be "fee only."

It's important to note that each of the Seven Cs evaluation traits in this exercise are compensation-method neutral. In other words, a particular compensation method does not preclude the financial planning professional from adhering to the highest standards of each Seven C ideal.

When it comes to paying for any service, an important question that needs to be asked and answered is about value. Ask yourself the following: *Based on what I am learning about this potential LFA, do I believe I will receive the value I desire in a nonconflicted way at a fully disclosed cost that is reasonable compared to other services of the same type?*

Other costs to consider: custodian fees, transaction fees, and account termination fees.

- **Transparency.** How easy is it for you to see all costs you pay for the services provided? Ask the prospective adviser to show you examples of how and where all fees and costs are disclosed. There are an alarming number of people who have no idea of the total cost they are paying a financial adviser because the cost disclosures are not clear or available. Ask this: *What can I expect the total cost to be if I hire you?* Break the costs down as up-front, ongoing and back-end. Also ask these questions: *Why do you structure your fees as you do? What will I receive in exchange for the costs I pay?*

Request a written breakdown of services and costs. Generally, there are two primary service categories: financial planning (paid by an estimated hourly rate, a retainer, a flat fee, or included in the cost of investment management services) and investment management services (paid by an annual asset management fee—percentage of assets under management (AUM)—or paid by commission). *Ask if there are reoccurring financial planning costs each year. Also ask if there are fee discounts depending on the amount of my money managed by the LFA.*

Request a sample of the adviser-client engagement agreement and read it as part of your homework. If you have questions or concerns, don't sign the agreement until you are satisfied.

MAKING THE GRADE

Evaluate Your Findings and Make Your Decision

Once you have completed the seven Cs assessment exercise and any other areas that are important to you, it's time to evaluate your findings and make a decision about hiring your LFA. Many people find it helpful to reevaluate every year or so to make sure their needs are continuing to be met in the best way possible.

Seven "Cs"	LFA Candidate #1	LFA Candidate #2	LFA Candidate #3
Evaluate and Grade:	Name: Firm:	Name: Firm:	Name: Firm:
Preinterview Investigation			
Character			
Commitment			
Communication			
Competence			
Connections			
Comprehensiveness			
Compensation			
Overall Grade			

Assign grade for each category as: A, B, C, D, or F

ADVISER EDGE

A 2015 survey by the Secure Retirement Institute, entitled *A New Perspective on Retirement Income*, reported the following:

- Individuals who work with paid financial professionals are more likely to have formal, written retirement plans and to be confident that they are on track with their retirement savings.
- Confidence in being able to live their desired lifestyle in retirement is higher among those working with paid financial

professionals, particularly for less-wealthy households.

- Among preretiree households with less than $500,000 in financial assets, there is a significant difference in subjective levels of retirement preparedness between those who work with financial professionals and those who do not work with financial professionals.
- Half of all consumers who work with a financial professional have worked with their adviser for more than five years.

A GREAT LIFETIME FINANCIAL ADVISER, MORE THAN A FINANCIAL PLAN PROVIDER OR INVESTMENT MANAGER

I believe the process of creating and implementing a written financial plan will be the deciding factor in whether people get to add the letters "in" in front of the word "dependent" when they describe their financial status in retirement. That said, I also know from my own experience that the hallmark of a great LFA versus someone who is merely providing a financial planning service is in the attention given to things that happen outside the financial planning process. Sadly, genuine care in serving the needs of people in all service industries seems to be a rare commodity these days. Hey, is it just me or have you noticed too that the quality of customer service has fallen dramatically since firms began announcing they are recording your call for training and quality purposes?

All professional financial planners will promise exceptional service and attention to detail when you first are introduced. I've never met a financial adviser whose marketing message is "ordinary service is our goal" or "we work hard to be mediocre." Yet I have met many people who describe their relationship with their financial adviser as average at best. Never settle for less than exceptional. The really good ones are out there, and you deserve it!

I most enjoy reading real stories of LFAs who do the unexpected for their clients' families. Those are things like showing up at important events when invited or remembering a favorite restaurant for a birthday or anniversary celebration. Even things like an unsolicited, out-of-the-blue phone call (I prefer live voice over impersonal text or email) really go a long way in carrying the message of "I do care for more than just your money."

Chapter Fifteen

Funding and Protecting Your Retirement-Life Plan

"Would you tell me, please, which way I ought to go from here?" asked Alice.

"That depends a good deal on where you want to get to," said the Cat.

"I don't much care where—" said Alice.

"Then it doesn't matter which way you go," said the Cat.

"—so long as I get *somewhere*," Alice added as an explanation.

"Oh, you're sure to do that," said the Cat, "if you only walk long enough."

—Lewis Carroll, *Alice in Wonderland*

The art and science of financial planning assumes you *do care* and want to be somewhere (fun and purposeful) in retirement and not "just keep walking (working) in place," feeling no closer to your goal. For those who choose to avoid the risks of going it alone, you and your LFA can create a road map (financial plan) that very well could be the difference between arriving at Wonderland versus Neverland!

CREATING A COMPREHENSIVE FINANCIAL PLAN FOR RETIREMENT

How will you know if your plan is comprehensive? You'll know it when you see it. A professional comprehensive retirement financial plan will include and address each of the areas detailed below.

Part A: Financial Plan Creation—What It Includes

- A written life plan exercise describing what you aspire to be, do, and have during each facet of your retirement lifestyle
- An accurate, detailed statement of your net worth (assets minus liabilities)
- Retirement lifestyle monthly funding budget—projected or actual. Includes both fixed and variable expenses. Also includes all expenses classified as essential (needs) or nonessential (wants, wishes, or dreams). See the homework assignment in this chapter.
- A statement of assumptions used to create projections for funding all your future goals and the reasons why these assumptions were selected. An agreement to review and update all assumptions annually. Discussed in greater detail in this chapter.
- A retirement income and expense projection (annual cash flow report) that illustrates a year-by-year potential surplus or deficit, and the resulting value of your retirement assets. Your needs, wants, and wishes are prioritized and are assigned money values and approximate time for realization.
- A timing and optimization assessment of your entitlement income such as Social Security and pension benefits. This assessment answers the question—based on the client's unique circumstances—of the ideal time to begin Social Security and/ or pension benefits.

Part B: Funding the Plan—What It Includes

Preretirement Accumulation Phase
- An investment policy statement that defines asset allocation goals, investment amounts, types, and objectives, investment time line, cost, and emotional comfort level.
- A preretired, asset accumulation and debt-reduction priority plan.
- Prioritize investing for short-, mid-, and long-term goals and debt repayments.

Retirement Distribution Phase
- Selection of an investment-income distribution strategy with the best probability of successfully funding the entire retirement lifetime period (several examples discussed in this chapter)
- An income tax planning review that highlights optimum (tax-advantaged) investment distribution during retirement years

Part C: Protecting the Plan—What It Includes

- Create a financial, economic, and personal-risk profile. Assess the real and potential-risk impact level as high, medium, or low. Determine a risk-mitigation strategy of ignore, assume, avoid, or transfer, beginning with all potential high-impact risks.
- Develop a written estate plan that provides for an efficient management and distribution of estate property. Include these valid, written documents: will, power of attorney, medical directive, and trust (if applicable).
  - Review all beneficiary designations
  - Complete a life insurance-needs review

Part D: Implementing and Maintaining the Plan

- The plan should have an agreed-upon timeframe to implement each action, a review of all costs (if any) associated with each action, and who is responsible for the implementation of each action—you, your adviser, or a third party.
- The plans should have a timetable for regular reviews to monitor progress, update information, and adjust actions accordingly. A review meeting should be held at least annually.

All components of a written retirement financial plan are important. Two in particular, however, are critical to minimizing the risk of early asset depletion: an accurate retirement monthly spending budget and the chosen assumptions that are used for unknown variables that affect the plan results. If you are creating your retirement financial plan with a financial adviser, he or she will undoubtedly request that you complete a monthly expense assessment exercise and assist you in deciding which financial plan assumptions will be used in your plan. Completing these two exercises prior to a formal planning engagement will provide important input to your planning process.

RETIREMENT-LIFESTYLE MONTHLY EXPENSE REPORT

Sadly, most people are not accustomed to completing a monthly expense budget during their working years. Did you ever hear this joke: "I still have unused checks in my checkbook, so I can't be out of money!" It's important to think of a spending budget not as a restrictive spending allowance but as a tool to take control of what you spend and save. Not doing so is the financial equivalent of driving your car with a broken fuel gauge. You don't know if you have enough gas (income) to make it to your destination (next paycheck), hoping to not hear a dreaded sputtering sound before you arrive.

Maintaining financial independence during your retirement-recess years is the most important financial goal you will ever have and is contingent on an accurate estimate of the monthly costs to fund your desired lifestyle. Once completed, if your retirement budget indicates that the lifestyle you envision requires a level of assets greater than you currently have or can realistically accumulate before your retirement date, modifications of your goals will need to be considered. Occasionally, there are those who have acquired assets in excess of those required for their lifestyle goal aspirations. For this fortunate group, a retirement spending budget will include additional lifetime-spending and estate-gifting allowances.

Homework:

Create your monthly retirement spending Report.

Begin the monthly expense exercise by listing current, actual monthly living expenses and future, retirement monthly living expenses in current dollar values. If you don't have budget worksheets, I have provided blank worksheets in the *Retirement Recess Homework/Exercise Workbook* (available for download at www.retirementrecess.com.) for this exercise. Label each expense as either essential (important to your retirement lifestyle) or nonessential (nice, but you could live without it). Also, indicate if the expense is fixed (no affected by inflation) or variable. I've included some discussion about retired cost-of-living-increase assumptions later in this chapter. Your checking account register or bank statement and credit card statements are excellent sources for identifying budget expense information. Highlight any monthly expense amounts that will be eliminated before or during retirement such as a mortgage and auto payments—list the age when they will be paid in full. Also include expenses you expect to add to your monthly budget during your retirement-recess years, if any, and at what age they will appear and for how long.

The following are examples of average costs in 2009 values for the most common expenses in retirement—compliments of the Bureau of Labor Statistics. Notice how the amounts are age sensitive and, with the exception of health-care costs, tend to decrease over time.

Average Costs for Essential Expenses in Retirement

Essential Expenses	Age: 55-64	Age: 65-74	Age: 75 +
Housing	16,991	14,462	11,811
Transportation	8,323	7,033	3,631
Food	6,743	5,950	4,377
Health care	3,895	4,906	4,779
Insurance	6,793	2,669	964
Clothing and Personal	1,591	1,322	793
Miscellaneous	5,221	4,117	3,734
Total Essential Exp.	$52,463	$42,957	$31,676

Expenses are for an individual. For a two-person household, double the expenses except housing and transportation costs. Source: US Bureau of Labor Statistics, October 6, 2009.

Next, list any lump-sum expenditures and assign priorities as needs, wants, and wishes. Examples could be a new auto (need), unless it's a Porsche (wish), second home (wish), exotic travel (wish), home improvements (want), etc. Estimate a dollar value for each and a timeframe as to when you would like to achieve each goal. Your listed "needs" by definition are the things that must happen, such as replacing an automobile to have dependable transportation. "Wants" are important but not essential, such as a vacation home or extended-travel trip. "Wishes" are not essential to your well-being, but they could be realized if you were to receive an unexpected windfall of cash in the future. A "wish" is something that may come true at that point—maybe a world-tour family vacation.

It's important to be as accurate and inclusive as you can when completing this exercise. Most people find it is easier to cut back on some expenses (nonessential) if your budget calculations are indicating a shortage of funds rather than trying to stretch dollars further for added expenses after the retirement-recess bell has rung.

FUTURE VALUES ASSUMPTIONS

Planning is all about the future, and the future by its very nature is unknown unless you are a psychic, in which case planning isn't necessary because you already know the result. For those of us who don't know what the tomorrows of our future will bring, retirement financial planning requires us to make assumptions about unknown future values such as cost of living, life expectancy, investment returns, and other factors in order to accurately evaluate how different strategies will affect a desired retirement outcome. Some variables are known—like your desired retirement age. Other future variables will need to be guesstimated as accurately as possible and then updated regularly for greater accuracy.

The Rule of Guesstimation

When you plan for the future, assumptions must be made about the unknowns that will, in time, affect a desired outcome. For example, when you plan a vacation, you make assumptions about the weather forecast and pack your bags accordingly. If the forecast turns out to be accurate, your clothing will be appropriate. If not, you'll be shopping to accommodate the actual weather during your trip.

The financial and emotional planning process of funding your retirement-recess lifestyle involves making several assumptions about factors whose actual future values are unknown. Because we can't know the future with exact certainty, we must estimate what we think future values will be. In other words, we guess. It might be a bit unsettling to discover that your financial plan—the blueprint to funding your future lifestyle, the primary planning tool that helps define the line between financial independence and dependence on others—is based on guesstimations. Only time will confirm the accuracy of the assumptions used to define your financial destiny. Although the past is no guarantee of future results, we can presume that past values provide reasonable expectations and a starting point to help estimate future outcomes—give or take a bit.

The rule of guesstimation states that if you wish to increase the probability of your assumptions being accurate, use relatively conservative, in-the-middle guesstimates. This way, if you err, it's on the side of being more conservative rather than wildly overstated or understated.

The great unknown of all planning variables (and the one very important to the success of your retirement-recess plan) is your lifetime expiration date. If we only could know for sure when our time would be up, we could plan with 100 percent accuracy to spend down our last dollar on our last day and bounce the check to the undertaker! For most of us, life's end remains a mystery.

Based solely on historic trends, many people seriously underestimate their life expectancy when planning for their retirement years. I have lost count of the number of people I have met over the years who have said, "I had no idea I was going to live this long." If you underestimate your life expectancy, the risk of outliving your money rises (longevity risk). Or, if you overguesstimate your expected remaining lifetime and you experience an earlier-than-anticipated demise, you may have lived more frugally than might have been necessary (frugality risk? I just made that up.) Of course, in this case you won't know or care, but your family might.

If you, like most people, are uncertain of the age you should use as your life expectancy, there is an exercise you can complete to help refine your guesstimation for this number.

Homework:

Determine your life expectancy goal.

Go online to: https://apps.goldensoncenter.uconn.edu/HLEC/ and access the healthy life expectancy calculator developed by the Goldenson Center at the University of Connecticut.

This is a very good free life expectancy calculator that is not affiliated with a commercial site. In addition to providing useful insights about how your habits and lifestyle affect your longevity, a prediction about future unhealthy years is also provided. This is an estimate of years within your total remaining life expectancy when you may experience serious health concerns. A reminder: For most folks, remaining life-expectancy years are not always healthy years. Feel free to add or subtract a few years from the estimate if you desire to modify the results. Personally, I don't want my financial planner to knock me off until age one hundred (for planning purposes) even though my life expectancy projection is a few years less than my goal. Once an optimist, always an optimist!

In addition to life-expectancy age, the following is a list of the most common assumptions used in a financial plan, ranging from conservative to more-aggressive assumptions:

Common Assumptions Used in Financial Planning for Retirement

Variable	Conservative	Moderate	Aggressive
Mortality Age Note: Assuming younger mortality ages are considered more aggressive due to heightened risk of underestimating your actual mortality date, resulting in not having enough money to fund the years beyond your estimate.	95 or higher	85-95	85 or lower
Annual Inflation Percentage— Living Expenses	5% or higher	3–4%	2% or lower
Annual Inflation Percentage—Medical	7% or higher	5–6%	3–4%
Investment Performance: (*) Five-Year Average Growth (Stocks)	5% or lower	6–7%	8% or higher
Income (Bonds)	2% or lower	3–4%	5% or higher
Cash (Money Market)	0.5% or lower	1–2%	2% or higher
Systematic Investment Withdrawal Percentage	3% or lower	4%	5% or higher
Tax Expense: Fed and State	30% or higher	25%	20% or lower

(*) It's important to note that the difference between actual historic long-term investment return averages of common stocks, bonds, and cash are significantly different than generally accepted long-term future projected returns for the same asset classes. The reason is this: Based on current economic, political, and financial factors, most "crystal ball" oracles predict future performance of stocks, bonds, and cash to be lower than those earned in past decades. In the above table, the "aggressive" assumptions generally reflect long-term historic averages while "conservative" assumptions reflect generally accepted future estimates.

TAKE NOTE

BASED SOLELY ON HISTORIC TRENDS, MANY PEOPLE SERIOUSLY UNDERESTIMATE THEIR LIFE EXPECTANCY WHEN PLANNING FOR THEIR RETIREMENT YEARS.

Be advised that while using conservative planning assumptions increases the probability of actual occurrence, they also increase the capital required to meet a particular goal when other factors are considered equal. More aggressive assumptions reduce the required amount of money to meet a goal, but if actual results are less than anticipated, an underfunded situation may occur. Using a moderate (middle) set of assumptions provides a balanced approach for projecting results. An actively managed plan readjusts variables each year to reflect actual results.

TAKE NOTE

WHEN IT COMES TO CHOOSING A VALUE FOR YOUR GUESSTIMATION OF UNKNOWN FACTORS WITHIN YOUR FINANCIAL PLAN, IF YOU ARE UNCERTAIN ABOUT WHICH VALUE TO CHOOSE FROM A RANGE OF POSSIBILITIES, CHOOSE THE MIDDLE VALUE.

Professional opinions vary greatly about what assumption values should be used for planning purposes. The assumption values listed above are for illustration purposes only. You and your LFA should discuss and decide what guesstimates are appropriate for your situation and temperament. A summary table of assumptions used to create your financial plan should accompany your planning documents for future reference.

If your monthly retirement expenses are not already adjusted to compensate for inflationary increases for the years between now and your retirement-age goal, make this adjustment for planning purposes. Some monthly expenses may be fixed amounts, such as fixed rate mortgage payments and/or auto loan payments, and they should not be inflated.

As previously discussed, your inflation-adjusted monthly expense total is an extremely important component in the retirement-recess planning process. A common rule of thumb is to take 60–80 percent of current salary and inflate by an annual inflation assumption multiplied by the number of years until you retire.

Example:

Current Household Annual Salary:	$ 80,000
Adjusted Annual Retirement Income:	$ 56,000 (70%)
Future Adjusted Retirement Income:	$ 75,260*

*($56,000 x 1.03 compounded three percent inflation assumption each year for a retirement beginning in ten years.)

However, I know of many people who are living comfortably in retirement on much less than these percentages. I also know others who require a higher amount of income to fund their desired lifestyle. I recommend you use an actual expense budget calculation as discussed previously rather than a percentage of salary to determine the real cost to fund your retirement. The other two components to determine the cost of your retirement recess are your life expectancy (previously assigned as homework) and your annual cost-of-living increase (inflation) during your retirement years.

COST-OF-LIVING ADJUSTMENT (COLA) IN RETIREMENT

It's a common planning practice to extend a level annual inflation percentage (usually 3 percent) throughout the entire retirement period. Others will adjust annual cost-of-living increases more dynamically based on lifestyle stages (early, middle, and late)—or, if you like, go-go, slow-go, and no-go stages—in retirement. There is evidence that indicates that for many retirees, actual monthly household expenses tend to increase less in the later stages of their retirement-lifestyle years than in the initial phase. Others hold to the reasoning that although some inflation-prone expenses decrease in later years (travel), other inflation-sensitive expenses (health-care services) increase in later years so that the total budget differences balance out. You must decide how conservative or aggressive this assumption should be for your unique situation. Remember to review this and all planning variables at least annually and adjust your financial plan accordingly.

RULES OF THUMB

Rules of thumb are statements that generalize a value that works as a starting point. Usually the statement goes something like this: "As a rule of thumb, we use (x-value) in our planning assumptions." These generalizations may or may not be appropriate for your specific planning needs. Common rules of thumb include:

- You will need 60–80 percent of your preretirement working income in retirement.
- Subtract your current age from one hundred. The answer is the maximum percentage of your investment plan that should be invested in stocks.
- Assume 4 percent is a "safe" annual investment withdrawal rate.
- Assume a 3 percent annual inflation rate throughout all your retirement years.

TAKE NOTE

RULES OF THUMB HOLD TRUE FOR SOME BUT NOT FOR ALL PEOPLE.
MAKE SURE THE RULES OF THUMB YOU CHOOSE DON'T BECOME
THE RULES OF DUMB!

ASSIGNMENT

Homework:
Create your financial plan assumptions list.

Using the Financial Plan Assumption Values worksheet in the Retirement Recess Homework Workbook, *complete your retirement plan assumptions list.*

Important: The Statement of Financial Planning Assumed Values should be reviewed and adjusted annually. In actual practice, I rarely see this occur.

RETIREMENT INVESTMENT INCOME—A TRANSITION FROM A SINGLE-FOCUSED TO A MULTIPURPOSE INVESTMENT PLAN.

For many years during your working life, you have been seeking a high return *on* your money (single-focused, inflation-protected capital growth). As retirement recess nears, it's time to consider employing an investment strategy that includes a return *of* your money—income for the near term and capital growth (continued return *on* your money) for later income needs—or a multipurpose investment plan.

The main objective of a single-focused investment strategy is to grow money over time through relentlessly paying yourself first each month and employing the "eighth wonder of the world"—compounding returns—so one day you can be employment free. The three objectives of the multipurpose retirement investment plan are the following:

- Provide a stable current income stream to supplement other retirement-income sources (offering liquidity and flexibility) so you don't need to continue to work for income
- Produce security of principal (diversification, professional management, discipline) so you don't need to seek work for income as a result of being unprotected during the next financial crisis du jour
- Create inflation protection for future income needs (capital growth) so you don't need to return to work five years later when inflation has raised your cost of living beyond the ability of fixed-income sources to keep pace

There are several possible strategies to accomplish these objectives and make the transition from a single-focused investment plan of growth to a multipurpose strategy of growth with current income. Your exact retirement investment plan will depend on your individual situation, including age, retirement-income needs, amount in retirement accounts, other income assets, and retirement entitlement benefits such as Social Security and pensions.

The following are examples of common retirement-income distribution strategies.

FIXED-AMOUNT DISTRIBUTION STRATEGY—AKA PLAYING CHICKEN

This strategy structures retirement-income distributions by choosing an annual fixed percentage distribution amount redeemed from an initial investment balance, usually monthly. The initial income amount is fixed except for increases in subsequent years by an assumed inflation percentage (historically 3 percent). The primary investment account can consist of a single mutual fund or a more complex investment allocation account made up of several investment funds with diversified investment objectives. The selected percentage of income withdrawal is usually based on what is deemed "safe" or having a high probability of not depleting the investment balance prior to a planned termination date (most often the assumed life expectancy).

This optimal (safe) income distribution strategy's roots can be traced back to the 1990s, when actual market returns were historically higher and life expectancy was shorter. In the past, it was not uncommon to see assumed "safe" income withdrawal rates as high as 8-plus percent per year! After the 2002–2003 and 2007–2009 financial market crises and the resulting interest rate decline, a 4 percent per year maximum income distribution rate became the generally accepted upper limit for "safe" income withdrawals from retirement investment accounts. Even so, recent studies using projected future stock market returns rather than historic performance values challenge these assumptions. Some findings reveal that given enough prolonged negative economic and market pressures, even a 4 percent income distribution rate may fail to keep the primary investment account from depleting itself over longer life expectancies. Using a lower percentage distribution (1–3 percent) increases the likelihood of not depleting principal dollars during a multi-decade lifetime payout period. However, lower distribution rates, although safer from the perils of early depletion, also reduce the net income the recipient will receive.

A major emotional challenge for the account owner when using this strategy occurs while watching the account value drop during periodic market declines. In addition, the account owner is simultaneously withdrawing an increasing (adjusted for inflation) monthly income amount from the declining retirement account or accounts. This feels a bit like playing chicken with your retirement investment savings, hoping that financial markets adjust upward before you spend down to a point where you may not be able to recover before you crash and burn. Hypothetical investment illustrations covering many years of actual past market performance may prove a proposed systematic withdrawal strategy successful. But the account owner is not hypothetical; he or she is real, with real emotions. Success for this strategy requires the investment owner to practice faith that financial markets, and thus the investment account, will recover from any periodic decline over time. History reveals that during a thirty-year run of retirement recess, an account holder may see five or more periods of substantial decline and recovery. In reality, most investors find it hard to sit on their hands and do nothing during such difficult times without assurances from a professional financial adviser. For those who give in to fear created by a perception that a temporary loss in value is permanent, cashing out during such declines turns an emotionally difficult situation into a full-blown, run-for-the-hills reality. In other words, they headed for the ditch (cashing out) before risking a head-on collision with what they believed to be a fatal permanent loss.

Those calmer retirees who do not abandon their income strategy during financial market declines historically see their investment account value recover as markets recoup their losses and move to new higher valuations. With no guarantees that history will again repeat itself, income recipients of this strategy must believe that stock market recovery will always follow periodic financial market declines. Since the future is not known until it occurs, the question remains: How much time (weeks, months, years) must pass before beliefs are vindicated and the account owner sees the investment account regain its value?

VARIABLE-INCOME DISTRIBUTION STRATEGY

Another multipurpose investment strategy involves using the inflation-adjusted, fixed-income distribution strategy discussed above, but with an important difference. Actual distributions are adjusted each year by multiplying a fixed percentage by the actual account value (variable) rather than using a fixed percentage of the initial fixed amount. It's called the inflation-adjusted, variable-income distribution strategy, also referred to as the endowment distribution strategy.

To reduce the threat of an excess distribution risk during periodic financial market declines, a modified *variable,* rather than fixed-income distribution strategy, is utilized. With this plan, the recipient adjusts his or her annual income percentage (for example, 4 percent) by the actual account value at the end of each year. This strategy is similar to the required minimum distribution (RMD) that IRA account owners are subjected to once they are over age seventy and a half and begin mandatory distributions. The only difference: the distribution percentage remains the same (example 4%) vs increased each year using the RMD method.

During negative financial market years, income shortfalls can be cured by adjusting household expenses for the deficit period or by redeeming funds from a "crash" cash reserve (for instance, a money market or high-yield savings account) or using other standby reserve sources such as a reverse mortgage. During years when income surpluses are experienced due to excess market gains, reserves can be built up, a reverse mortgage balance can be paid down (if applicable), and/or monthly expenses can be increased.

When utilized correctly, the inflation-adjusted, variable-income distribution strategy can greatly reduce the risk of excess distributions from your primary investment account(s) in down market years. This approach also provides some emotional relief to the account holder during periodic market declines. It does, however, require an annual review of account value and subsequent adjustment to the income distribution amount for the next year. Most users of this strategy withdraw the current year's adjusted-income amount as one lump sum and deposit it into a money market or high-yield savings account for monthly distributions of one-twelfth each for twelve months.

GUARANTEED-ANNUITY INCOME STRATEGY

This approach is sometimes referred to as a "personal pension." It resembles a traditional pension offered through an employer or government agency except that the guaranteed-annuity income plan is funded by the investor instead of the employer and is not connected to employment in any way.

This income strategy offers a lifetime-guaranteed income stream for a single or joint life expectancy. Similar to a traditional pension, the guaranteed-income payments are usually fixed (entailing an inflation risk) and the principal that provides the income payments is not available (causing a liquidity risk) to the account owner during the owner's lifetime or to the estate beneficiary when the owner dies. These two risks can be mitigated by adding extra features such as inflation, liquidity, and refund riders to the annuity account. Doing so will come at the cost of reduced income payments during the participant's lifetime.

The amount of income is determined by the age at which payments begin. This feature is also similar to another guaranteed retirement-income program—Social Security.

The following example compares two commencement ages, sixty and seventy-five, for a male requesting an immediate annuity payment for life from an insurance company. All other factors are equal, including the initial investment of $100,000. Income amounts for females may be slightly lower since they have longer life expectancies.

Monthly amount

Age	Life Only Income	Payout Rate*	Breakeven**
65	$ 541	6.49%	15.4 years
75	$ 741	8.90%	11.2 years

*Payout rate equals return of principal plus earned interest.
**Breakeven—years you must live and collect to receive your initial investment back via monthly payments received. (Note: Income payments are guaranteed to continue for annuitant's lifetime regardless of breakeven period.)

Now let's request the same income strategy but add a refund of unused principal upon death to the personal pension annuity owner. This income program will still remain illiquid during the lifetime of the participant.

Age	Life Income*	Payout Rate	Breakeven
65	$ 492	5.91%	16.9 years
75	$ 609	7.31%	13.7 years

*Refund: You receive this income for your lifetime. If you die before receiving an amount equal to the initial investment, your beneficiary will receive a lump sum equal to the remainder of the principal that has not yet been paid to you. This amount is not adjusted for cost of living (COLA).

Much like deciding the age to take life only income payments from other guaranteed retirement-income programs such as Social Security or pension, deciding when to begin taking income from a guaranteed-income annuity program depends greatly on how long you believe you will live. The longer you wait to begin, the higher the benefit you receive for whatever lifetime remains.. Important exception: waiting past age seventy to begin Social Security income benefits provides no additional benefit.

Other considerations:
- Income payments received from guaranteed annuity programs include interest (taxable) and a return of principal, which is not taxable if the initial investment was made with nonqualified (after-tax) dollars.
- Guaranteed-income annuity programs are offered by many different insurance companies. Research both the income payment offers from several companies and the financial strength (financial-strength risk) of each before you invest money.

VARIABLE ANNUITY WITH GUARANTEED-INCOME RIDER

A variable annuity is a contract with an insurance company using an assortment of mutual funds as investment choices in addition to a fixed-interest option. Unlike a traditional fixed-rate annuity as described above, the account value of a variable annuity will rise and fall with market conditions depending on the asset allocation chosen by the account owner. A guaranteed-income rider can be added at an additional cost that creates a guaranteed income stream for the life of the account owner and, if elected, for the life of a spouse.

Actual guaranteed-for-life income amounts are dependent on the variable account balance and elected-income rider options. Variable-annuity programs make available several options to customize both income and death-benefit guarantees. Each option has a benefit and a cost if elected. Some restrictions may apply. It is important for anyone considering this investment retirement-income choice to obtain a thorough explanation of benefits, costs, and restrictions before investing. Variable annuities are sold by prospectus, a legal document outlining all features, benefits, and costs.

OTHER POSSIBLE RETIREMENT-INCOME STRATEGIES

- Real estate rental income
- Business owner sale or ongoing-revenue income
- Reverse mortgage
- Royalties
- Stock dividends

Guaranteed income sources in addition to fixed- and variable-rate annuities:

- Certificates of deposit
- Bond interest (if bond principal is held to maturity)
- Index annuity account

An advantage of using a guaranteed-income source is receiving uninterrupted income regardless of current financial-market conditions. Disadvantages include lack of inflation protection and relatively low-interest yields. Also, these choices may lack liquidity and flexibility.

TAKE NOTE

WITH FEW EXCEPTIONS, WHEN YOU SEE THE WORD "GUARANTEE" CONNECTED TO INCOME, THE ADDED COST IS HIGHER INFLATION RISK AND LIQUIDITY RISK. BOTH OF THESE RISKS, LEFT UNMITIGATED, MAY INCREASE THE POTENTIAL OF AN ACCELERATED SPEND DOWN OF OTHER ASSETS OVER A MULTIDECADE RETIREMENT.

WHICH RETIREMENT-INCOME STRATEGY IS BEST?

Once again, the answer depends on you. Specifically, it depends on your age, current assets, debts, life expectancy assumptions, other income sources, income tax status, and other important factors.

Many people choose to use a combination of income sources rather than relying on one or two strategies. An example is matching essential expenses with guaranteed-income sources such as Social Security, pension, and income-annuity programs, and then using fixed or variable investment-income strategies for nonessential expenses. The thinking here is that the things you must pay for (essential expenses) are funded with guaranteed-for-life income amounts that are not dependent on the economy or financial markets. The expenses that are nonessential (wants or wishes) are funded by inflation-protected, financial-market-driven (variable) sources. Nonessential expenses can be curtailed or expanded depending on the year-by-year performance of the financial markets.

EXTRA CREDIT

GO TO WWW.RETIREMENTRECESS.COM/RETIRE-READY-RESOURCE-CENTER AND STUDY RETIREMENT INCOME-STRATEGY COMPARISONS.

AVOID ALL-OR-NOTHING INVESTMENT GOAL EXCHANGES

There are many nonfinancial examples in which a gradual transition is more appropriate than an abrupt one. For example, when a commercial airplane approaches its destination, you begin to feel the transition from cruising speed and altitude to the approach and landing sequence prior to the wheels touching down. The plane gradually slows and begins its descent. The cabin is prepared, and an announce-ment about landing is made. Pilots or the auto pilots land the aircraft using "small moves" rather than abrupt actions to safely guide the airplane onto the runway and to its terminal gate.

Think of the transition from accumulating assets during your work-ing years to your retirement lifetime in a similar way. As you approach your retirement age (destination), you begin to ready your investment accounts for periodic distributions in the near-term. This may equate to reallocating a portion of your assets to provide a steady stream of income to supplement other sources at some point. This first income-distribution destination is not the final stop along your retirement track. A portion of your retirement assets needs to fly on to future distribu-tion points as you travel through what hopefully is a long and reward-ing retirement.

A potentially hazardous (inflation-risk) mistake is to reposition 100 percent of your retirement assets from capital appreciation (single-focused growth objective) assets into principal-safe investments (sta-ble-value objective) consisting of CDs, short-term Treasuries, and/or money market accounts upon or just before reaching your initial retirement age. Unless you need 100 percent of your entire retire-ment account available for income supplement initially, this is a prime example of trading one risk (periodic financial-market volatility risk) for other core risks such as inflation, lifestyle, and excess-distribution risk. Remember, you are expecting to consume income not just in the short term but for many years in the future—a possible three-to four-decade period.

FINANCIAL PLAN SCENARIO RESULTS

Rather than guessing or hoping that your actual financial planning results will be optimal, a financial planning scenario can be produced based on your current assets and liabilities, income, lifestyle goals, and chosen assumptions.

With the aid of professional financial planning software, all pertinent information discussed previously can be entered into a computer program, and a variety of stress-test scenarios can be created to evaluate how your planning goals react under difficult situations. It is at this point that many do-it-yourselfers discover they lack the necessary resources to produce a detailed financial plan scenario result that professional retirement planners make available to their paying clients. If you are a do-it-yourselfer and don't feel comfortable completing this assignment without professional help, consider hiring a retirement-planning specialist by the hour to complete this important work with you.

Financial Planning "Bewares"

- Beware of "free" retirement planning calculators. With few exceptions, they tend to produce insufficient results. You get what you pay for.
- Beware of assumptions that fall out of the range of those discussed earlier.
- Beware of using average annual returns versus actual year-by-year returns for investment-return assumptions, especially if you are planning to withdraw income in the beginning years of your retirement from an account invested at least in part in the stock market.

- Beware of one-and-done planning exercises. Many financial exercises need to be revisited and updated at least annually. Your life is not static; neither is your plan.
- Beware of the one-investment-product solution to retirement financial planning. You can own the perfect investment (if it existed) and still run out of money in retirement without the benefits of comprehensive planning.
- Beware of believing you can create a comprehensive financial plan on a napkin or an index card. Some journalists claim professional financial planners intentionally make planning difficult to justify their costs. Personally, I wish planning for a three-decade retirement was simpler. It is what it is. I do know the cost of being shortsighted due to ignorance or laziness is far greater than the cost of being thorough.

Homework:
Produce a written retirement-plan scenario result.

With the aid of a financial adviser or on your own, create a retirement-plan scenario result that accomplishes your retirement-income goal with a low probability of depleting your retirement assets prior to the end of your life-expectancy assumption.

REVIEWING YOUR FINANCIAL-PLANNING RESULTS

If the final analysis of your retirement-lifestyle goals and financial resources concludes that you have a shortfall—meaning under the current scenario there is a high probability of depleting assets before your assumed mortality age, don't despair. The power of planning before rather than after a premature savings spend down gives you choices to alter your lifestyle and/or change your strategy before you commit to a plan that might fail.

If a shortfall exists in your plan, review and recheck all data and assumptions. Rerun the plan. If after careful review, all assumptions and data are correct and a shortfall still exists, consider the following strategies.

- **Delay retirement recess:** Postpone your retirement recess until your plan indicates you have sufficient funds to last your entire remaining life expectancy. Consider the quip: "My plan works with a high probability of success if I retire at age sixty-five and die at sixty-seven!" Extending your employment years a bit further can buy you time to get all your retirement-recess preparation homework finished and grow your retirement-income pool of money a bit more. Delaying your retirement date also reduces the number of years your supplemental retirement savings will need to provide support (assuming your mortality age remains the same). However, as we have discussed, working longer increases employment risk.

- **Recess now, but on a lower-lifestyle budget:** Decrease your retirement-recess income needs by reviewing and cutting non-essential expenses from your budget. Be careful not to reduce essential living expenses below the point of what is necessary to support the basic needs of your retirement lifestyle. Underestimating your actual living costs won't ensure anything except increasing core risks, specifically lifestyle risk and excessive-withdrawal risk, which can contribute to an early demise of your retirement recess. Also, consider changing some of your "needs" to "wants" and "wishes" if possible. If things work out better than planned, you can reinclude these goals into your plan as "needs" later.

- **Save more/incur less debt:** Choose to save additional earned income during your working years for later retirement-recess income. If you have the ability to do so, defer larger portions of your paychecks into accounts earmarked as retirement-recess income assets. With less time, you won't enjoy the benefit of long-term compound earnings as younger savers do, but accumulating additional principal dollars will increase income potential as you convert these additional savings into guaranteed-income sources later. This option provides a great opportunity for younger workers to bring their retirement savings amount up to an appropriate level and avoid having to consider the first two options later. Consider paying off debts (home mortgage, auto) more aggressively prior to your retirement date. Rerunning retirement-planning scenarios with mortgages retired before you do often makes a substantial difference in the results. Refrain from taking on new long-term debts if your ideal planning-scenario result is already flashing yellow or red.

TAKE NOTE

DON'T RISK YOUR FUTURE FINANCIAL SECURITY BY SPENDING MONEY EARLY IN RETIREMENT ON "WISHES" THAT YOU MAY LATER WISH YOU HADN'T WISHED FOR.

In summary, you have learned that the main purpose of a comprehensive retirement financial plan is twofold: It identifies the needed capital resources to fully fund a lifestyle goal based on a set of chosen assumptions, including a detailed spending budget; and it provides an assessment and mitigation plan for potential financial, economic, and personal core risks (retirement income security killers) that can cause an early spend down of assets over your retirement recess. Its effectiveness in carrying out this main two-fold purpose is dependent on the accuracy of information utilized, the inclusiveness of data, and the degree to which recommended actions are carried out. Done well, a retirement financial plan increases the overall quality of a retirement-recess experience and reduces the two fears greater than dying: Running out of money before running out of lifetime and not remaining relevant during your entire retirement-recess journey.

The next chapter explores specific actions to help gauge how ready you are for retirement recess. It is a review of the topics we've covered throughout this book. Enjoy the ride!

Chapter Sixteen

Planning for the Journey: One-Way or Round-Trip Ticket?

Whenever someone asks me, "When can I retire?"— I always respond with an immediate answer: "Today!" After pausing for a moment, I continue, "You might run out of money tomorrow, but you can certainly retire today." Successful retirement planning is about funding the entire lifestyle journey, not just a portion of it. Having enough money to get you only halfway is simply not acceptable. The retirement journey you aspire to enjoy requires a round-trip ticket. The first leg of the trip is to accumulate sufficient assets to provide an uninterrupted, inflation-proof, after-tax income stream to finance the second leg of the trip—a distribution strategy for your remaining life. Whether you travel first class or coach through your retirement-recess years depends on your resolve to save during your gainful working years and the thoroughness of preparation before your journey begins.

In 1961, President John F. Kennedy challenged the nation to land a man on the moon by the end of the decade. Although he did not live to witness his great challenge become a reality, as a nation we did accomplish the goal several months prior to the end of the 1960s. As a visionary, JFK predicted, "We will succeed not because it is easy, but because it is hard."

When we decided to go to the moon, it took years of preparation to determine what was required prior to July 16, 1969, when that big Saturn V rocket beneath Apollo 11 lifted off from its launchpad destined for the lunar surface and man's first walk on the moon. It's important to remember that the goal of the mission wasn't just to land men on the moon. It was to land on the moon *and* return safely to Earth. In other words, the astronauts had round-trip tickets—at least they hoped they did. Halfway was simply not an acceptable option.

The same is true when planning for the successful mission of a multi-decade financially independent retirement. It takes years of preparation before you launch into your retirement lifestyle. The goal isn't to just reach retirement. The goal is to calculate and acquire the financial resources required to get you all the way through what you hope to be the most fulfilling years of your entire life voyage. Neil Armstrong, the commander of Apollo 11, said that even after his historic walk on the moon, watching the Earth get bigger in the window of his tiny spacecraft as it hurtled toward home was a most welcome sight. Think of your quest for financial independence as the means to transport you securely from retirement liftoff, through decades of retirement-recess adventure, and—after a successful retirement recess mission—arriving at whatever image is in your homecoming window.

RETIREMENT-RECESS COUNTDOWN

Recalling what you have learned thus far, let's count down the years of preparation needed to fully enjoy retirement recess for grown-ups. The following chronological countdown includes a collection of examples of traits and actions of those who are ready for round-trip retirement.

T-Minus Thirty to Forty Years before the Retirement-Recess Bell

Your future recess destination is nearly a generation away. It's difficult to imagine a place so distant, but you sense that just as your current age has arrived in a flash, so too will your retirement destination emerge quickly into fuller view.

You enjoy your young adult independence, so you decide to begin saving on your own to reduce future financial dependency on others. Leveraging the power of compounding interest over time, using the discipline of paying yourself first out of each paycheck, and investing in a diversified, growth-oriented portfolio can lead to your serious-money retirement account beginning to increase rapidly in value. Your contemporaries who wait even just a few years (procrastination risk) to begin their pay-self-first program find they must save a much greater amount to arrive at the same destination as you.

You commit 10–15 percent of what you earn to a tax-deferred or tax-free employer retirement program such as a 401(k) or Roth 401(k) plan, collecting 100 percent of your employer's matching dollars into your retirement account. If no employer plan is available, you establish and fully fund a tax-deferred IRA or tax-free Roth IRA—plus an additional investment account expressly for your retirement, which receives investments in addition to the IRA maximum contribution.

You diversify your retirement accounts with investment-fund choices that historically exceed the long-term increases in your future cost of living. Your long-term investment goal is not trying to "beat the market" but to beat inflation and income-tax costs (a goal of about five percent a year combined). Any investment returns above this goal will help improve your margin of success.

You face occasional emotional distress during periods of market volatility that cause your account values to decline. Although it may feel like you are going backward, these periodic setbacks provide powerful thrust for the next leg of financial-market growth. You rely on the principle of "financial certainty"—trading the safety of current account value, especially during periodic market declines, for the certainty of future inflation-protected income for life. You embrace the rewards that await those who are disciplined about staying on course over the long-term—especially during financially turbulent times.

Since your goal is to convert accumulated growth investments into wage-replacement income dollars in the far-off future, you elect to reinvest all dividends and capital gains, buying additional shares of your investment, which increases future income potential.

T-Minus Twenty to Thirty Years before the Recess Bell Rings

You are focusing most of your time on career and family and beginning to discover nonmonetary values in life that are important to you. You begin to seek professional advice beyond the work associate in the next cubicle about your growing retirement-savings nest egg. You ask important questions that deserve professional, unbiased responses: Am I investing correctly? Will it be enough? What else should be considered? You realize your growing wealth not only holds the key to your financial independence, but if managed well, it can become a legacy passed on to future generations—some of whom may be sitting around the dinner table with you right now. You help your kids finish their homework and begin to wonder what homework you should be completing to avoid becoming financially dependent on them in your later years. You wonder who, if anyone, should help you with your retirement-planning assignments. You learn about estate planning, and you create a will, power of attorney, and medical will. You analyze the financial risk of an untimely death or disability and purchase enough life and disability income insurance to financially provide for your family should one of these events occur. You base your insurance purchase amounts on your actual need and not how much premium you can afford to pay.

T-Minus Ten to Twenty Years before the Retirement Recess Bell

Life is busy. If you have children, they are late teens or young adults. Your attention and checkbook focuses on helping them with college costs. You find yourself trying to strike a balance between the demands of work, family, and personal time. You catch yourself thinking about an interest that you enjoy but feel rushed when you try to pursue it. You ask yourself if there is something greater for your life than just your current career. You ponder whether your future retirement might not only be a resignation from something, but also an invitation to pursue something different, something greater, something deeper.

Your retirement-lifestyle vision begins to feel like a graduation from the classroom of your working years—a commencement to a new way of living that combines your dream job with long periods of playtime spent with family, friends, or just yourself. It won't be all work or play, but periods of work and recess like when you were in grade school. You begin to comprehend the word "recreation" as "re–creation."

Unlike many of your contemporaries, you live within your financial means, paying off debts rapidly and thus increasing your credit score ratings, which reduces future borrowing costs when you do need a loan. When short-term emergencies occur, you access your ready-cash-reserve savings rather than taking on more debt or committing the mortal retirement sin of borrowing from your retirement account(s). Your home mortgage is scheduled to be paid in full near your retirement date.

Through the financial planning process, you have discovered the financial planning "homework" assignments that need to be completed to arrive at this new destination within your time frame and not someone else's. Like the gravity of the moon, as you travel closer to your retirement age, you begin to feel the draw of this lifestyle pulling you toward it.

Once you are over age fifty, you are eligible to begin making additional catch-up contributions, and you are aware of the current-year limits. Here are the limits as of 2019, with the additional amounts possible for those over the age of fifty:

- 401(k)—an additional $6,000 above the $19,000 limit
- 403(b)—an additional $6,000 above the $19,000 limit (plus an additional $3,000 per year for five years if certain conditions are met)
- Traditional IRA—an additional $1,000 above the $6,000 limit
- SIMPLE IRA—an additional $3,000 above the $13,000 limit
- Roth IRA—an additional $1,000 above the $6,000 limit

At age fifty-five and older, the following applies:

- The 10 percent early withdrawal penalty ends within 401(k) plans for terminated employees
  - Upon separation of service from an employer at age fifty-five or older, you may elect to take early distributions from your 401(k) without being subject to the 10 percent early withdrawal penalty. Distributions are taxed at your ordinary income tax rates in the year of distribution.

- If you are planning to request distributions from a former employer's 401(k) plan prior to age fifty-nine and a half, you learn it may be beneficial for you to maintain the former 401(k) account rather than rolling it over into an IRA. Requesting pre-fifty-nine-and-a-half distributions from a former employer plan will not trigger the 10 percent early withdrawal tax penalty. An IRA does not have the pre-fifty-nine-and-a-half age waiver of the early withdrawal penalty unless certain conditions are met.
- If applicable, you are eligible to make additional health savings account (HSA) contributions
  - Make additional deductible catch-up contributions of $1,000 above the limit ($3,500 for singles and $7,000 for families in 2019) if you maintain a health savings account (HSA).

T-Minus Five to Ten Years before the Retirement Recess Bell

You begin to feel the nearness of your new lifestyle vision. While still employed, you practice play periods for extended periods of time. You have identified all the stumbling blocks that may impede your financial success and possess a written plan to manage each risk. You individually, or with the help of your retirement financial adviser, have written a plan of action to manage high-impact core risks to your future retirement income and have implemented strategies to transfer away or avoid each. You commit to review retirement income security killers (RISK) at least annually.

At age fifty-nine and a half and older the following applies:
- The 10 percent tax penalty ends for early IRA withdrawals.
  - You can begin taking withdrawals from your retirement plan

accounts and/or traditional IRA accounts without being subject to the 10 percent early withdrawal penalty. All distributions will, however, be subject to ordinary income taxes.

- The contributions and earnings component of a qualified Roth IRA distribution are tax- and penalty-free if both of the following apply:
  - The distribution is taken after a period of five years beginning January 1 of the tax year the first contribution was made.
  - *And* the owner attains age fifty-nine and a half, becomes disabled, dies, or uses the distribution for a first-time home purchase (maximum $10,000).

Roth IRAs do allow for distributions of principal investments to be distributed at any age without income tax or early penalty. All earnings taken prior to age fifty-nine and a half are subject to income tax and penalties.

T-Minus Under Five Years before the Retirement-Recess Bell

You have finished your financial homework by creating a detailed, written budget identifying both your essential and nonessential expenses throughout your retirement-recess lifetime. You have refined your estimates and age goals of entitlement-income sources such as Social Security and pensions, if applicable. You have determined the conversion amount needed from retirement assets to create additional guaranteed-for-life income to pay for essential expenses. On your own or with the help of your lifetime financial adviser, you begin the transition from a growth, single-focused investment objective to a multistrategy plan consisting of growth, income, and preservation objectives.

You have accumulated a sufficient pool of discretionary savings to pay for nonessential expenses during your retirement-recess play periods.

At age sixty-two, this is the situation:

- Early but reduced Social Security benefits are available to those who qualify.
  - You can start receiving Social Security income benefits, but they will be reduced by a fraction of a percentage point for each month before your full retirement age.
  - Reduced Social Security benefits are for your lifetime and affect spousal income and survivor benefits for their lifetimes.
- At age sixty-two you are eligible to apply for a reverse mortgage as a strategy to turn home equity into retirement income.

At age sixty-five, this is the situation:

- The 20 percent penalty ends for HSA nonqualified medical-expense withdrawals.
  - Distributions used for nonqualified medical expenses from a health savings account (HSA) are only subject to income tax and will no longer be subject to a 20 percent early withdrawal penalty.
- Eligibility for Medicare kicks in.
  - Medicare eligibility begins at age sixty-five. If you are already receiving Social Security at age sixty-five, you will be automatically enrolled in Medicare. If you are not receiving Social Security benefits at age sixty-five, you are encouraged to enroll three months prior to age sixty-five. If you fail to enroll at the time you were eligible, the cost of Medicare Part B can go up 10 percent for each full twelve-month

period not enrolled. This penalty applies for as long as you continue to have Medicare Part B.

- Additional standard deductions apply on your tax returns.
  - If you are sixty-five or older, not married, and not filing as a qualified widow(er), you can receive an additional $1,300 standard deduction on your federal income taxes. All other taxpayers who are sixty-five and older receive an additional $1,650 standard deduction (2019 data).
- Full retirement age (FRA) for some Social Security recipients (if born in 1942 or before) applies.

At age sixty-six, this is the situation:

Full retirement age (FRA) for some Social Security recipients (if born in 1943 through 1959) applies.

At age sixty-seven, this is the situation:

Full retirement age (FRA) for some Social Security recipients (if born in 1960 or after) applies.

At age seventy, this is the situation:

The maximum postponed Social Security benefit is available.

- If Social Security benefits are postponed, you become eligible for the maximum Social Security benefit at age seventy. Those who wait to age seventy to collect receive a remaining lifetime 8 percent annual increase plus any cost-of-living increases based on their full retirement age (FRA) amount.

At age seventy and a half, this is the situation:

IRA required minimum distributions (RMD) commence. (In other words, you can't take it with you—at least not tax-free).

- You are required to start making minimum distributions from traditional IRAs and other retirement-plan accounts by April 1 of the year after you turn seventy and a half. Each year after the age of seventy and a half, all RMDs must be made by December 31. Participants still employed may delay the first minimum distribution of their employee account until April 1 of the year following the termination of employment. Fifty percent penalties may apply if an RMD is not taken on time. Ouch!

Blast off. You have finished all your homework prior to your retirement-recess liftoff date. In doing so, you feel confident that you have sufficient resources to last throughout the entire journey. Additionally, you have considered the risks you might encounter along the way and have mitigated their potential negative effect on your trip. Risks like unexpected health costs and the always-possible threat of a financial market meltdown are always looming. Strategic planning helps reduce these perils and the potential of a delayed retirement blastoff while building confidence for smooth traveling throughout your entire journey. Remember, you are planning for a round-trip experience. Halfway is not an option!

Conclusion

A Retirement-Recess
Life Well Lived

The room was silent as an attractive woman dressed in black business attire slowly approached the wooden podium positioned near the front of the room. As she arrived, she turned and paused for a moment. Scanning the room, she observed the crowded space filled with a diversity of people all waiting in silent anticipation. She fixed her eyes on the large portrait of an elderly but stately gentleman placed next to a spray of red roses and a lit single white candle. Then she began to speak.

"My name is Casey, and Carl was my grandfather. I can't remember ever blowing out a birthday candle or opening a Christmas gift when he wasn't present. He attended all my graduations and was front and center at my wedding. I still remember his trademark wink, which was his unique playful signature that always reminded me that life was not just for living, but for enjoying.

"Grandpa was fond of quaint little sayings that were simple in nature and wise in meaning. One he recited often was that "there is no present like time." I asked him once where that saying came from. He told me it was part of a rhyme from a children's book he read to my brother and me. I recently located the book. It is titled *Molly Moon's Hypnotic Time Travel Adventure*, and it's by Georgia Byng. I would like to share the remainder of the rhyme with you:

There's no time like the present,
No present like time.
And life can be over in the space of a rhyme.
There's no gift like friendship,
And no love like mine.
Give me your love to treasure through time.

"Grandpa was there for the birth of our two children and most recently returned with our oldest son, Chris, from a week-long camping trip in the mountains of Colorado. He winced when he told us upon his return that the ground has gotten harder as he's gotten older."

The silence of the audience was broken with brief laughter. Casey continued. "While I was growing up, Grandpa often shared that he thought of his life in retirement as recess for grown-ups. He told me he finished all his homework before his recess time began, about the same time that I was born. He explained that as a result, he could afford to spend his best years with people he truly loved and who loved him.

"Just because my grandfather was at recess didn't mean he didn't have important work to do long after he retired from his primary career. His contribution as founder and director of Second Chance Animal Shelter, a place dedicated to the mission of matching abandoned and abused dogs and cats with their new forever families was more than a job to him. He said it was what God intended him to do and that his prior career was just a stepping stone to his "God job."

"Driven by his love for animals, Carl and the dedicated folks at Second Chance Shelter placed hundreds of dogs and cats with new forever families. Without his care, these animals would have met a tragic end. Looking around the room, just like the animals he loved, there is not a person here today who has not been touched and in many ways 'saved' by my grandfather."

Casey wiped a tear from the corner of her eye and flashed a faint smile while saying, "We laughed often and much, my Grandpa and I. He taught me many things that you can't learn from books or even parents. It wasn't his knowledge, but his gentle, unhurried, and steadfast wisdom I remember the most. He always seemed wise beyond his years. He had time for me. He was my advocate from my earliest remembrance.

"I miss my grandpa dearly. Yet I am so grateful for his long life, the memories of all the times we shared, and most importantly, that he shared his recess years with you and me. Yes, there is no present like time."

* * *

Carl had a well-planned life vision of what he wanted to be, do and have during what turned out to be a thirty-eight-year retirement period. His lifetime financial adviser helped Carl create a living financial plan that never became outdated. When financial risks threatened his income flow, there was a meeting of the minds and a plan to follow. When Carl got cancer in his later years, there was a meeting and a plan to follow. And finally, when Carl died, his plan did not. His financial legacy lives on for his family and future generations, thanks to his plan.

The best financial plans function undetectable in the background of lives lived fully throughout retirement years. They provide the means for lifetime goals to manifest and flourish undistracted from financial worries. They are seamless, reliable, effective, and flexible. A retirement lifetime well lived is a lifetime well planned for.

How about you? When the retirement recess bell rings, will you be ready?

Go confidently in the direction of your dreams.
Live the life you have imagined.
—Henry David Thoreau